Divorce and Remarriage

Divorce and Remarriage

by
Ken Stewart, D. Min.

HARRISON HOUSE
Tulsa, Oklahoma

5th Printing
Over 25,000 in Print

Divorce and Remarriage
ISBN 0-89274-343-3
Copyright © 1984 by Family Worship Center
P. O. Box 690240
Tulsa, Oklahoma 74169

Published by Harrison House, Inc.
P. O. Box 35035
Tulsa, Oklahoma 74153

Contents

Introduction

And it came to pass, that when Jesus had finished these sayings, he departed from Galilee, and came into the coasts of Judaea beyond Jordan;

And great multitudes followed him; and he healed them there.

The Pharisees also came unto him, tempting him, and saying unto him, Is it lawful for a man to put away his wife for every cause?

And he answered and said unto them, Have ye not read, that he which made them at the beginning made them male and female,

And said, For this cause shall a man leave father and mother, and shall cleave to his wife; and they twain shall be one flesh?

Wherefore they are no more twain, but one flesh. What therefore God hath joined together, let not man put asunder.

Matthew 19:1-6

There is hardly a family in America today which has not been touched directly or indirectly by divorce. This is as true for those in the Church as for those on the outside. Yet there seems to be so little solid scriptural teaching on this vital subject.

The scriptures quoted above are without doubt some of the most controversial in the entire Bible. In fact, this whole subject tends to be controversial. Therefore, before getting into a study of it, I would like to make clear my purpose and motive in addressing it.

First of all, let me point out that I am not divorced. I don't say that to boast, but as a simple statement of fact. I would also emphasize that with the help of God I never will be divorced. I am very happily married and have every intention of remaining so.

So then, what I have to say on this subject is not written to justify something I have done, or ever intend to do. It is written for the purpose of shedding light on a subject which for too long has been either ignored or misunderstood. I want to help those in the Church of Jesus Christ who find themselves caught in this unfortunate situation. I hope to be able to provide them with some clear-cut guidelines from the Word of God.

Now you may ask, "If you've never been divorced yourself, what qualifies you to teach on the subject?"

A person's qualification to teach something never comes from experience. Despite the popular saying, experience is not the best teacher—in fact, it is often the worst. There is another old saying: Experience keeps a dear school, but fools will learn in no other. I trust that neither of us is a fool who can only learn by experiencing failure firsthand.

No, an individual's qualification to teach comes from his knowledge of the subject. And the best source of information on the subject of marriage and divorce is not personal experience, but the Word of God, the testimony of the One Who designed and instituted marriage in the first place. So I can't speak from experience, but even if I could, I wouldn't do it. My experience would only give you something to relate to, something to identify with, and you really don't need to identify with other people's failures. When you do that, you are identifying with the wrong thing. You need to hear the truth. And God's Word is the ulti-mate truth on this subject.

Secondly, I believe I am more qualified to teach on this subject without having been divorced than I would be if I had experienced it myself because I am not biased in my viewpoint of it. I can approach the topic without having to overcome personal feelings or emotions about it.

I have no "hang-ups" about divorce one way or the other. Nor do I have "an ax to grind." I am not trying to prove a point. I do not approach the subject with any preconceived notions about divorce, adultery, fornication, remarriage or any such thing. I am free to face and accept the truth whatever it might be. I am not setting out to find scriptures to try to "prove" any particular opinion or point of view. I simply want to share with you the honest truth about this matter from the inspired Word of God so you too may experience the joy and fullness God wants you to have, the joy and fullness I have known in my own blessed marriage.

It is not my intention or goal to be controversial, sensational, or negative. I am not trying to "stir up" something. On the contrary, I am trying to settle things down. It is not my desire to break up marriages; rather, I want to save marriages!

My wife and I have been appointed by God, set in the Body of Christ, for the specific purpose of instructing God's people in family relationships. We are endeavoring with everything in us to fulfill that calling. I don't want anyone to read this message and mistakenly think they have found in it an excuse or license to get a divorce.

I want to make one point clear right from the beginning: *I am against divorce.* According to Malachi 2:16, God hates divorce. So do I!

So the purpose of this study is not to encourage divorce, nor to encourage divorced people to remarry. I would simply like to call attention to some truths from the Word of God for you to consider *before* you make a decision on either of these issues. It is my prayer that as you read, you will be open to the Holy Spirit of God so He can reveal to you His divine will for *you* personally in regard to these crucial areas of Christian living. God bless you!

—Dr. Ken Stewart

1

Is Divorce a Sin?

The Spirit of the Lord is upon me, because he hath anointed me to preach the gospel to the poor; he hath sent me to heal the brokenhearted, to preach deliverance to the captives, and recovering of sight to the blind, to set at liberty them that are bruised,

To preach the acceptable year of the Lord.

Luke 4:18,19

If there is any scripture passage that should be applied to the divorced and the remarried, it is this one. There are millions of poor, brokenhearted, bound, blind, bruised divorced people in our nation. Some of them have remarried, others have not. Sad to say, rather than setting at liberty these that are bruised, the Church as a whole has put them into greater bondage, has added to the hurt, the blindness, the bruises. This is not intended as an indictment against the Church—it is merely an observation.

Like you, I have seen so many people hurt, crushed, and destroyed over this matter of divorce and remarriage that, frankly, before God I have no choice: I have to speak out. This is the reason I have done so in the past and the reason I will continue to do so. God's people must know the truth on this vital issue. For it is the truth that sets people free—not church tradition.

11

There are many Christians who think the Church knows the truth about divorce and remarriage. Based on the bondage and controversy so prevalent today in this particular area, it is obvious to me that the truth of this matter is far from being fully known.

I have spent literally hundreds of hours counseling with people. Divorced people. Remarried people. Some have been remarried once, others twice, some three times, four times, five times and even more. (One lady whom I counseled was in her *seventh* marriage!) When I shared with these people the truth of God's Word, some of them would look across my desk at me and flatly declare, "Yes, I know that's what the Bible says, but I believe...." And what they believed was usually the very thing that was holding them in bondage. It is the truth that sets people free, not popular opinion, even if that opinion is held by an entire church or denomination.

What I have to share with you in these pages is truth, not opinion or doctrine. There are many churches and ministers who declare today that divorce is a sin. That is nothing new. As a child, I remember hearing that pronouncement repeated from the pulpit time and time again: "Don't get a divorce. Divorce is wrong. Divorce is a sin." That message was preached over and over until about half the Church wound up divorced.

Then, faced with the indisputable fact that, despite all the sermons and pronouncements, church members were indeed getting divorced, the preachers began declaring, "Don't remarry. Remarriage is wrong. Remarriage is a sin," until all the divorced people got remarried. Now the Church doesn't know what to say:

"Well, we're not quite sure about this matter of divorce. Sometimes marriages just don't work out. So if yours didn't, don't feel bad—it happens to a lot of people." And it must be admitted that indeed there is "a lot of that going around these days"!

But what happens if one of these divorced Christians asks his or her minister to perform a marriage ceremony? More than likely, the first thing the preacher is going to ask is not "Are you saved?" but "Have you ever been married before?" If the answer is yes, the divorced person will probably be informed to go down the street to another church, or to the Justice of the Peace!

In other words, it is all right to get divorced nowadays—even to get remarried—just as long as it's not done in the church house. What hypocrisy!

Of course, those who are divorced or remarried can still attend church—they just can't take any part in it. I have actually read books of church doctrine which state that those who are divorced or remarried are forbidden to sing in the choir, teach Sunday school, serve as deacons or elders or ushers, or to fulfill any role of leadership or responsibility in the church. The only thing such people are allowed to do is *tithe*—that's always permitted!

It is no wonder people are confused. Why would any pastor who loves and cares about his people not be willing to accept them when they have made a mistake, forgive their past failures, and work to help them put their broken lives back together and go on to live a happy, productive life? He would do that for any church member who had become an alcoholic or drug addict or even a thief—provided, of course, the repentant sinner wasn't either divorced or remarried!

It doesn't make sense, does it? Yet that very thing is going on in many of our churches today. No wonder the world doesn't take the Church seriously. Look at the kind of hypocritical games we play.

The church world has made a legalistic thing out of the whole matter of divorce, remarriage and adultery. (I am linking the three together because that is the way they are usually connected in people's minds.) We've made the divorce issue so legalistic that absolutely no one could keep the laws we've established.

Yet with all our legalism we still have no solution to the problem. Doesn't that tell us something about our "cure"? Basically we have just shrugged the whole thing off thinking, "Well, that's another one of those things we'll understand by and by, when we all get to heaven."

But we won't need the answer then. There won't be any divorce problem in heaven. We can't put it off any longer—we need answers here and now.

Is divorce a sin? Is remarriage a sin? Is there ever a situation in which divorce or remarriage is not a sin? If a person gets a divorce, is he or she guilty of adultery? Is the former mate guilty of adultery? Even if the divorce was involuntary? Even if he or she never remarries? Is it forbidden to a Christian to remarry after a divorce or to marry a divorced person?

These are questions which must be answered if Christians are ever to function in the freedom and fullness which God desires.

Is Sin a Thing?

Now let me put this question to you. Suppose my marriage ends in divorce for some reason other than immorality on the part of my wife. Suppose she divorces me against my will. If divorce is truly a sin, am I then doomed to live in sin the rest of my life?

Some people would say, "Oh, no. If your wife divorces you, you won't be living in sin—*as long as you don't remarry!*"

Wonderful. Now I'm forced to make a decision between remaining single the rest of my life or "living in sin." Does that seem fair to you? It doesn't to me.

The problem is, we don't understand what sin really is. Most people think sin is a *thing.*

Years ago, if someone had asked me what sin is I would have answered, "Smoking, drinking, dancing, bowling, tennis, football games, movies and mixed bathing." (I would have probably also said it was a sin for men to wear Bermuda shorts and for women to cut their hair.)

To me sin was a thing, an act, something a person *does* because that was what I had been taught. In Sunday school many times our children are told, "These things are sin...." and there follows a whole list of things or activities. So naturally most people grow up thinking that if we can somehow ever get rid of all these bad things, then we can get rid of sin.

There are a lot of people who don't smoke, drink, dance, or do any of this, yet who are sinners. We may call them good, clean, moral, upright citizens. But the truth is, they are really sinners!

There will be thousands of such people in hell—people who have never smoked a cigarette in their lives, or got drunk on Vodka martinis, or danced the boogie-woogie or watched John Wayne on the silver screen. (I'm quite sure that Judas Iscariot never did any of this!) Why will they spend eternity in hell? It certainly won't be because they were guilty of doing any of these hideous "things."

For generations we Christians have made an erroneous assumption. We have thought that sin is a thing. I was led to believe that divorce was one of the worst of sins. (Did you ever attend a church which taught that some sins were worse than others? I did.) Drinking was worse than smoking. Taking drugs was worse than drinking. Adultery was worse than taking drugs. Divorce was worse than adultery. But worst of all was *remarriage!* That was an unpardonable sin.

No one actually came right out and said that in so many words, of course. But it came out just the same: "If you get a divorce or remarry, we'll love you, brother. We'll be sorry for you. But you won't be able to be a deacon anymore, or take up the offering, or teach a Sunday school class, or sing in the choir, or...." In other words, "God will forgive you, but we won't!"

What Is Sin?

Faced with such a list of sin-things, I finally reached a point in my life where I had to find out from the Word of God just what sin really is. What I discovered I would like to share with you. I think it will provide a fresh new perspective on this whole confused issue of divorce.

What is sin? How can it be recognized and defined?

In my study, I found three things about sin that are very important:

1. Sin is selfish.

In Galatians 5:19-21 we are given a list of what the Bible calls "works of the flesh": **Adultery, fornication, uncleanness,. lasciviousness, idolatry, witchcraft, hatred, variance, emulation, wrath, strife, sedition, heresies, envyings, murders, drunkenness, revellings, and such like....** If you will notice, there is not a thing on this list that is not selfish. "Works of the flesh" are selfish. That is the one thing you can say about sin that is absolute. Sin is selfish.

In fact, that is how sin got started. In Isaiah 14:13,14 we read Lucifer's (Satan's) boast: **...I will ascend into heaven, I will exalt my throne above the stars of God: I will sit also upon the mount of the congregation, in the sides of the north: I will ascend above the heights of the clouds; I will....** *I will, I will, I will.*

So to determine if anything is a sin, the first question to be asked is, is it selfish?

Now let me ask you a question. What is selfish about a woman cutting her hair? Take the list of things we have traditionally called "sin" and go down it asking yourself, is this selfish? That should make it clear which things are truly sin and which are not.

Someone might ask, "Well, what's selfish about smoking or drinking?"

The answer is simple. Smoking and drinking are unhealthy. They destroy the body which God gave man, the temple of His Holy Spirit. Is it selfish to knowingly destroy God's temple on the grounds that "it's my body and I'll do with it as I please"?

2. Sin is anything that displeases or hurts God.

Now take your list of things. Go down it and ask yourself again, is it selfish? If it is, you'll find that it also hurts God—it displeases Him.

Our bodies are the temple of the Holy Ghost. It displeases God, it hurts Him, for us to destroy His temple, because that's where He lives.

Hebrews 11:6 tells us: **But without faith it is impossible to please Him** (God)**....** What pleases God then? Faith. Faith *pleases* God. Romans 14:23 says: **...for whatsoever is not of faith is sin.** Well, if faith pleases God (without faith it is impossible to please Him), and if whatever is not of faith is sin, can't we say that anything that displeases God is sin? That's fairly simple, isn't it?

3. Sin is a decision.

I was always taught that sin is a thing, and one of those things is a *thought.* I was told that if I had a wrong thought, I had sinned. Thank God, that's not true!

Back then, I didn't know that the only arena in which Satan can operate is the arena of the mind. Many of the thoughts people have mistakenly assumed to be *theirs* have been nothing more than things Satan had spoken to their minds. People have said to themselves, "Dear God, where did that thought come from?

How sinful of me!'' They have started repenting of something they assumed to be their thought, something they considered a sin, when in fact it was nothing more than one of the devil's tricks. They repented of something which the devil had done. That's the worst deception of all!

Instead of repenting, what they should have done was resist the devil and he would have fled from them.

Sin is a decision, not a thought.

In Matthew 5:27-30 Jesus makes some startling statements. He talks about a man looking on a woman to lust after her. He says that when a man does that, he has committed adultery with her already in his heart. First John 3:15 talks about hatred being the same as murder.

Let me clarify these statements for you. In Matthew 5, I believe Jesus was saying that when a man looks upon a woman and *makes the decision that given the opportunity he would commit adultery with her*, that decision is accounted to him as sin. Likewise, when a man looks at his brother and *makes the decision that he hates him enough to kill him*, that man has already committed murder in his heart.

Sin is determined at the point of decision.

Under the Mosaic Law, a person had to do something to sin. Sin was an act. In order to sin, a person had to steal something, commit adultery, murder someone, or perform some other unlawful act. And, having broken the law, he also had to do something to be forgiven. What did he have to do to receive forgiveness? According to the Law, he had to make an animal sacrifice. Since sin was an act, forgiveness was conditioned upon an act of repentance. The whole thing was dependent upon man. If he did not perform the sacrifice, he was still guilty of the offense. That's the way the Law worked.

Under the New Covenant, sin occurs at the moment of decision—not at the moment of action.

"Oh, but I thought we Christians had a new and better covenant."

We do. Under the New Covenant all we have to do to be forgiven is to make the decision to accept the forgiveness that is already provided for us through the shed blood of the Lord Jesus Christ. The sacrifice has already been made, once and for all. It only remains for us to receive the forgiveness that is already ours through Him. Just as we sin when we *decide* to do something selfish or displeasing to God, so also we are forgiven when we *decide* to repent of that decision.

So then we can now define sin: *Sin is a selfish decision that displeases God.*

What Is Marriage?

Let's think together for a moment. Given this definition of sin, is divorce sin? Is remarriage? Well, it is obvious that they both meet at least one of the requirements for sin in that they are both decisions. But are they automatically selfish decisions, which are displeasing to God? If so, then they are indeed sin. If not, or if we are not absolutely sure in every case, then perhaps we have been too hasty in judging either them or those affected by them.

In the past we have not fully understood the subject of divorce, due in part to our misunderstanding of what marriage really is. The dictionary defines marriage as ''the state of being married; wedlock; matrimony; the act of marrying; the rite or form used in marrying; *any close or intimate union.*''

I'd like to take a closer look at this last definition. If we accept this as our definition of marriage, then it is no wonder the world has developed a sort of ''easy-come, easy-go'' attitude toward marriage and divorce. To them, marriage is just another ''close relationship,'' similar to those with friends or special acquaintances. This makes divorce just a definitive parting of two persons intimate at one time who now have decided for one reason or another to go their separate ways. In other words, we might say that divorce could be defined as simply a state of no longer being married. In that light, it doesn't seem so bad.

But now let me define marriage scripturally: *Marriage is the* **spiritual** *uniting of a man and a woman.*

In Genesis 2:18 we read that God said, **It is not good that the man should be alone; I will make him an help meet for him.** Then in verse 24 after God had brought the man and woman together, He declared: **Therefore shall a man leave his father and his mother, and shall cleave unto his wife: and they shall be *one* flesh.**

So then, Biblically speaking, marriage is the uniting of a man and a woman before God so that in His eyes they become one flesh. What do we mean one flesh? One in purpose, in motive, and in goals.

No, this doesn't mean that one or the other loses his or her personal identity. There is a common misconception prevalent today: ''I don't want to get married because if I do I'll lose my self-identity; I won't be *me* anymore!'' Well, there are some people who would do themselves and everyone else a great favor if they would lose some of their precious self-identity —(self-centeredness is a better word for it!)—and become concerned about something or someone besides themselves. No one is self-sufficient. Like Adam, we all need a ''help meet,'' someone to share all of life's experiences with us, someone with whom we can become one.

In marriage a man and woman actually become one in spirit. Now this is vitally important. The things that happen in life that are truly meaningful, that have real value, that really count, are those things that occur first in the spirit of a person. If you understand the Word of God at all, you understand this statement.

For example, if you seek to receive physical healing in your flesh, ultimately you will do so because you have received it first in your spirit. This is a spiritual law. Proverbs 23:7 says of a person, **As he thinketh in his heart** (spirit)**, so is he.** Jesus taught that whenever a person prays for something, if he believes in his heart (spirit) that he has already received it, then he will have it (physically). (Mark 11:23,24.) The spirit gets involved first. Once something has occurred in the spiritual realm (on the inside of a person), then sooner or later it will become manifest in the physical realm (on the outside).

Over and over the Bible says that in marriage the two become one *flesh*. What does that indicate? That they have already become one *spirit*. That's the reason Jesus said in Matthew 19:6: **What God hath joined**

together, let not man put asunder. God does not join the flesh of man with the flesh of a woman—they do that themselves. That is not marriage. It is simply the manifestation or expression of marriage. True marriage, true union, occurs when God joins the spirit of a man with the spirit of a woman.

How does that happen? Well, if you are a born-again Christian, how did your spirit become one with the Spirit of God? Was it not by what you believed in your heart and confessed with your mouth? When you believed the Word in your heart and confessed it with your mouth, you were reborn spiritually. Your spirit became one with God's Holy Spirit.

That's exactly what a wedding ceremony is supposed to be—a spiritual uniting. When a man and a woman believe something in their respective hearts, and come before God in the presence of witnesses to confess that belief, then what they jointly believe becomes *reality*. (Matt. 18:19.) Their two spirits become one spirit.

Then they become one flesh. In the past, we have spent far too much time concentrating on the physical union (or lack of it!) and not enough on the spiritual union. That is the reason we are seeing the tragic results of disharmony and disunion in the world today. Until people come to realize that marriage is a uniting of *spirits*, not just bodies, separation and divorce will continue to plague our society—in the Church and out of it.

After a couple becomes one *spirit*, and one *flesh*, they spend the rest of their married life working to become one *soul*. And that is where the problems usually begin to surface.

Of One Mind

Through the years of my ministry I have counseled with many, many married couples trying to discover where the root of their marital troubles lay. Many times in the process of counseling those about to get a divorce, they will tell me that their sex life is wonderful—they seem to be one in spirit and in flesh. Then where is the problem? In the soulish area, in the *mind*.

This is true in our relationship with God. That's the reason the Apostle John wrote: **Beloved, I wish above all things that thou mayest prosper and be in health, even as thy *soul* prospereth** (3 John 2). Many times it is not our spiritual relationship with God that hinders us from receiving from Him, nor is it our physical relationship with Him. Spiritually, we are just as much His children as ever. Physically, we are just as much a part of His Church as we ever were. Then where are we missing it? Well, where is the battleground in our stand against Satan? In the *mind*.

So it is with marriage. Marriage is a uniting of two spirit beings. That's why marriage ought to be between two people who are born again. What if a believer marries an unbeliever? The result is a live spirit "united" with a dead spirit. Would anyone want to marry a dead corpse? People don't go to the graveyard looking for a mate. Or do they? Many Christians are looking for a mate in the cemetery, among dead spirits. That is why the Apostle Paul warns Christians not to become **unequally yoked together with unbelievers** (2 Cor. 6:14).

The spiritual wedding before God should take care of the spiritual union. If it does, then that spiritual union should take care of the physical. So where is the problem? Why do things go wrong in marriage? Usually it is because the two partners have not yet become truly one in mind.

Once people grasp this truth, I believe we will begin to see a real difference in marriages. You see, a person's closest spiritual relationship is his relationship with God. But in marriage, he or she has the opportunity to become as close to another human being as to God. Viewed in that sense, marriage takes on a whole new dimension and significance.

According to Genesis 1:27 God created man in His own image. Then out of that which was created in the image of God, He took a rib and made a woman. **And Adam said, This is now bone of my bones, and flesh of my flesh: she shall be called Woman, because she was taken out of Man** (Gen. 2:23). It is easy to see here both the spiritual and physical unity of man and woman. But the problems Adam and Eve were to experience in their life together did not originate in either their spirits or their physical bodies. The real cause of their downfall was mental—they believed Satan rather than God. Their sin was a selfish decision (of the mind) that was displeasing (in disobedience) to God.

What Is Divorce?

The real significance of marriage is that in it a man and a woman become one with each other and one with their Creator. Therefore, in the eyes of God, marriage is forever. That may shock you, but I believe it to be the truth.

In the light of what we have just seen about the true nature of marriage, divorce takes on a different meaning. Divorce is not merely the dissolving of a partnership. Rather it is nothing less than the separation of two spirits which have been molded and melted together into one. Do you think they can be torn apart without harm either to one or both of the parties involved?

What we are dealing with here is not a partnership or joint effort. It is a spiritual union, second only to that spiritual union with God.

Can you see where divorce might be selfish? Displeasing to God? If marriage is a relationship between a husband and wife, patterned after that relationship between the Lord Jesus Christ and His Bride, the Church, then can anyone seriously contend that divorce is either unselfish or pleasing to God in any way?

When I am preaching this message in person, along about here someone usually asks me, "Well, if marriage is a spiritual union, what about unbelievers? If two unsaved people get married, are they really married?"

My answer would be, "Do they have spirits?"

"Yes, but they are dead spirits!"

"Then in their case, marriage is the uniting of two dead spirits, and divorce would be simply the separation of two dead spirits." Then I am always quick to point out, "But what those two spirits need is not *separation*, but *regeneration!* They don't need to separate. Just the opposite: they need to get together—with each other and with God!" This, of course, is the ultimate answer for any troubled marriage, inside the Church or out.

Causes of Divorce

The primary cause of divorce in our nation today is spiritual ignorance. There are probably more saved people in America today than ever before in our history, but there are also more unsaved people than ever before. This is not negativism—it's plain fact. And statistics have proven time and time again that the divorce rate among non-Christians far surpasses that among true believers.

The second greatest cause of divorce in America is lack of spiritual commitment. Many Christians just don't have the fruit of the spirit in evidence in their daily lives. The fruit of the spirit will have a real impact on a marriage. It will make marriage a success. But before people can experience the fruit, they have to experience the Spirit. And unfortunately vast numbers of Christians know nothing about the Spirit Who gave them birth.

Webster defines divorce as "a separation...to turn and go different ways... 1. in law, a legal dissolution of the bonds of matrimony, or *the formal separation of husband and wife by a court.* 2. separation; disunion of things closely united."[1] This definition is consistent with the dictionary definition of marriage. But, as far as I'm concerned, neither of them is any good because they make no mention of the true nature of either marriage or divorce.

---

[1]*Webster's New Twentieth Century Dictionary of the English Language Unabridged,* 2nd ed. s.v. "divorce."

As evidenced by this definition, we are conditioned to think of divorce as something that happens in a court, by law. Most people think you go to court to get a divorce. Nothing could be further from the truth. Divorce does not occur in a court, by law: divorce is something that occurs in the spirit, by sin. What takes place in court is simply a manifestation of what has *already* taken place in the spirits of the individuals involved.

There are a lot of people who are spiritually divorced and still legally married. Spiritually, they have torn their spirits apart whether they ever face each other physically in a courtroom or not.

There are many people who think that divorce has not occurred until they get to court. So they put off turning to God about their failing marriage until it is too late. There have been people who have come by my office for counseling on their way to the divorce court: "I've got to be in court in an hour and a half. Can you help me?" That's a little bit late to be seeking spiritual guidance!

People don't go to court to commit a crime—they end up there because they have committed a crime. So it is with divorce. Marriages aren't dissolved in a courtroom—that's just the place where the law duly recognizes something that has already taken place elsewhere.

Marriage is spiritual. Divorce is spiritual. We need to recognize that truth. We are spiritual beings. That means that the real you, the real me, is spirit; and anything that really matters in our lives is going to be spiritual. Oh, how we've overlooked that fact!

The most important thing in any person's life is his personal relationship with God. The second most important thing in any person's life is his relationship with his mate. That truth can be proven from the Word of God. We Christians have thought that our relationship with God was so awesome, so wonderful, so spiritual—and it is. Yet we've considered our relationship with our mate as just natural. We've looked upon it so carnally, so physically. No wonder there have been so many troubled marriages in the Church of Jesus Christ.

Your relationship with your mate is first of all spiritual. Until you realize that fact, your marriage can never be what you want it to be. But armed with that knowledge, combined with the power of the Holy Spirit of God, you can have an invincible marriage. Nothing will be able to put asunder **that which God hath joined together.**

2

God's Attitude
Toward Divorce

And this you do with double guilt; you cover the altar of the Lord with tears [shed by your unoffending wives, divorced by you that you might take heathen wives], and with your own weeping and crying out because the Lord does not regard your offering any more or accept it with favor at your hand.

Yet you ask, Why does He reject it? Because the Lord was witness [to the covenant made at your marriage] between you and the wife of your youth, against whom you have dealt treacherously and to whom you were faithless. Yet she is your companion and the wife of your covenant [made by your marriage vows].

And did not God make [you and your wife] one [flesh]? Did not One make you and preserve your spirit alive? And why did God make you two one? Because He sought a godly offspring [from your union]. Therefore take heed to yourselves, and let no one deal treacherously and be faithless to the wife of his youth.

For the Lord, the God of Israel, says: I hate divorce and marital separation, and him who covers his garment [his wife] with violence. Therefore keep a watch upon your spirit [that it may be controlled by My Spirit], that you deal not treacherously and faithlessly [with your marriage mate].

Malachi 2:13-16 AMP

This passage makes quite clear God's attitude toward divorce and marital separation. He *hates* it. Those are pretty strong words, and we would do well to take note of them.

But now let's look at this passage a little closer to see what else the Lord has to say about the subject of marriage and divorce.

Beginning with the thirteenth verse, we see that the prophet Malachi is explaining to the Jewish people of his day why God would no longer look with favor upon their sacrifices. The first thing we should notice from this passage is that God is a witness. Malachi tells the people that God will not accept their offerings "Because the Lord *was witness* [to the covenant made at your marriage] between you and the wife of your youth." As the timeworn words remind us: *Dearly beloved, we are gathered here today, **in the presence of God**, and in the face of this company....* God attends weddings.

Secondly, despite some teachings to the contrary, we see here that marriage is a covenant relationship: "...the Lord was witness [to *the covenant* made at your marriage] between you and the wife of your youth." *...to join this man and this woman **in the bonds** of holy matrimony....*

There are some people who teach that if two people are married and one of them is unfaithful to the other, that infidelity dissolves the marriage immediately. This is a false doctrine based on a misinterpretation of a statement made by Jesus in the nineteenth chapter of Matthew which we will examine later on.

But according to this passage, marriage is a covenant relationship between a husband and wife.

Even if one is unfaithful, the covenant still stands. Although the men of Israel were being unfaithful to their wives, God still refers to them as "your companion and the wife of your covenant." Behavior does not abolish relationship. Only a decision can do that.

The Residue of the Spirit

In verse fifteen the writer was careful to point out, "And did not God make [you and your wife] one [flesh]? Did not One make you and preserve your spirit alive?" Now in the *King James Version* this last sentence reads, **Yet had he** (God) **the residue of the spirit.** As I looked at this sentence I couldn't make sense out of it. I studied it in several different translations, but they seemed to vary so much I wasn't sure of its exact meaning. Finally, I went to the Lord: "Father, just what did You mean here? What is the **residue of the spirit?**" This is what I was shown.

God did make Adam and Eve one. But what He was really interested in was the residue of the spirit, that is, what is left over after everything else is taken away. In other words, God wasn't so concerned about making man and woman one *flesh;* He knew they would take care of that. What He was most concerned about was their becoming one *spirit* and the result or the fruit of that spiritual union.

You see, there are many people who make marriage vows. They believe in their heart, confess with their mouth, and become one with their mate. As we have said, this parallels what happens when we believe on Jesus in our heart, confess Him with our mouth, and become one with Him. But many times we have seen people make a commitment to the Lord, yet through the years give very little, if any, evidence that what they believed and confessed is actually true in their lives. Despite their supposed belief and confession, they seem to have no real relationship with God.

As human beings, we are inclined to judge a person's relationship with the Lord by what we see on the outside. What's wrong with that? Just this. When a person becomes a Christian, a new creature in Christ *on the inside*, things still remain that need to be dropped off *on the outside*. Once those carnal, fleshly things are removed or consumed, what's left—the residue—is purely spiritual. That person doesn't need to get saved again every time he fails to live up to his new inner nature, he just needs to make his ''walk'' come up to his ''talk.''

So it is with marriage. When two people come together before God, believing in their hearts and confessing with their mouths, they become spiritually united. But it's not just that union, that one moment, that concerns God. He is interested in seeing the two of them become outwardly what they have just believed and confessed themselves to be inwardly. They are then, and will continue to be, one spirit. Now they just need to begin to manifest in their thoughts, words, and deeds what has already taken place in their spirit. They need to strive to actually become what God has declared them to be—one identity. They are now each to put aside his or her independent, ''I-gotta-be-me'' attitude and spirit, and go to work to shape their new identity *together.*

Godly Offspring

In the *King James Version* of verse fifteen God warns: **Therefore take heed to your spirit, and let none**

deal treacherously against the wife of his youth.
Notice He doesn't say, "Take heed to your flesh."
There are many married couples today who are taking
heed only to their flesh.

Well, if God is more interested in the spirit, why
does He say over and over again that the two will
become one flesh?

To let us know that it's all right to be one flesh.
That's a by-product of being one spirit. Not everyone
understands that. Many people, especially Christians,
have serious "hang-ups" about the physical side of
marriage. They shouldn't. It was God Himself Who
designed our bodies for union. He planned for that just
as much as for our spiritual union. Throughout the
Bible He places His stamp of approval on the physical
union of man and wife. But it must be pointed out that
uniting bodies does not unite spirits, while united
spirits should result in united bodies. God planned it
that way.

Why? Why does God want married couples to
become one spiritually and physically? The answer is
found in verse fifteen: **And why did God make you
two one? Because He sought a godly offspring [from
your union].** You see, God wants you and your mate
to be one in spirit, body and soul, because the more
you become one the more likely you are to raise godly
children.

Can you imagine what would happen if even half
the population of the United States was saved, born
again, and filled with the Holy Spirit? Suppose we
could bring just 50 percent of the men and women in
America into the fullness of a relationship with God.
What do you think the next generation would be like?

This nation would be revolutionized—through the children! **Train up a child in the way he should go...** says Proverbs 22:6, **...and when he is old, he will not depart from it.** That is our hope for the future. That is God's hope and plan for the future of His people.

One in Spirit

God wants godly seed. We've not realized that our relationship with God has such a tremendous impact on our relationship with our mate. There are too many Christians today who think they can have a good relationship with their mate apart from their relationship with God. It can't be done. You are a spirit. The person you marry is a spirit. And if that spirit-to-spirit relationship is going to function properly, it will do so only because your relationship with God is right. There is no other way.

Then there are those who think that apart from their relationship with their mate they can have a good relationship with their children. That too is false. Your relationship with your children is heavily dependent upon your relationship with your mate. Someone has said that the best thing any man can do for his children is to love their mother. In the *King James Version* of Malachi 2:16 God says: **Take heed to your spirit, that ye deal not treacherously.** *Your* spirit is the one spirit you now share together with your mate. You must be careful to preserve the purity of that common spirit.

Does that mean that when two people become one spirit they cease to have a spirit of their own?

Someone once asked me, "Does that mean that when I get married, I'm going to lose my spirit?"

My answer was: "Did you lose your spirit when you became one with the Spirit of God? No, you're still there, aren't you? So you will be when you get married. The two of you will become one spirit, but you will each preserve his or her own individuality, just as you did when you became a Christian."

What I am talking about is a relationship—a close, personal, intimate relationship. You ought to be close to your marriage partner. You should be able to talk to each other freely, to communicate, to understand each other. Don't spend your life saying, "I can't understand that man; I can't understand that woman!" Change your confession. If you don't, you will end up getting exactly what you have been saying. Pray for your mate. Begin to bless him or her with wisdom and understanding. If you do, you'll be surprised how quickly you will start to reap the fruit of your lips.

God Hates Divorce

God hates divorce. Why? Because it reminds Him so much of what happened in the Garden of Eden when man put Him away. The first two people God made turned right around and divorced Him. Did you know that every time a divorce occurs, God is reminded of the time when He was put away? That hurts the heart of God.

You see, God never intended for a spiritual union to be broken. He did not intend for His union with Adam and Eve to be broken. God did not plan the fall of man.

Then why did He let Satan in the Garden?

God didn't let Satan in the Garden—Adam did. Even so, God trusted Adam and Eve. He believed in them. That's why their betrayal hurt Him so much. When you love and trust someone completely and are then put away by that person, it hurts. Don't think for a moment that the fall of man didn't hurt God. But did you notice that even though God was put away by His own creation, He didn't stop loving them?

God hates divorce. *But God loves divorced people!* That's the truth we need to keep before us at all times. God hates sin, but loves the sinner.

Although man rejected God, God did not reject man. Man divorced God, but God did not divorce man. He never stopped loving him. And because He loved man, God never gave up on him. He stayed after him. He didn't stop until He had done everything in His power to get the human race to love Him in return and come back to Him.

Thank God, our Father didn't give up on *you and me*. Let's not give up on our brothers and sisters who have divorced each other or Him.

God didn't have the attitude about divorce that so many married people have today. They just throw up their hands and quit: "Oh, well, we made a mistake. We missed it, we blew it. May as well get a divorce and get it over with."

Sometimes people do miss it. But often the problem is a lack of commitment. Today we have disposable dishes, disposable razors, disposable diapers, disposable clothes. Paper clothes. Just wear them once and throw them away. Our latest invention seems to be the disposable marriage. Try it awhile, and if it doesn't "work out," throw it away.

Leave and Cleave

But that's not God's idea. Divorce is not God's answer: **Therefore shall a man leave his father and his mother, and shall** *cleave* **unto his wife: and they shall be one flesh** (Gen. 2:24).

Wasn't that a strange thing for God to say at a time when there were no mothers or fathers to leave? There weren't even any husbands and wives yet, since this was the first marriage. God couldn't have been referring to Adam when He said this because Adam had no parents to leave. Obviously this was spoken and recorded for our benefit. Since it is found (in whole or in part) no less than four times in the Bible (Gen. 2:24; Matt. 19:5; Mark 10:6-9; Eph. 5:31), God must have wanted us to get the message: *We are to leave and cleave.*

Now the word *leave* is simple, we understand that. But what is this *cleave* business? In the Old Testament Hebrew, the word is *dabaq*, which *Strong's Concordance* defines as to "abide fast, cleave (fast together), follow close (hard after), be joined (together), keep (fast), overtake, pursue hard, stick, take." [1] In the New Testament Greek it is *proskollao*, which according to Strong means "to *glue to*, i.e. (fig.) to *adhere*:—cleave, join (self)." [2]

---

[1] James Strong, *The Exhaustive Concordance of the Bible* (Nashville: Abingdon, 1890), p. 29 of Heb. and Chald. Dictionary (hereafter cited as *Strong's*).

[2] Ibid., p. 61 of Greek Dictionary.

From these contexts and definitions it seems quite clear that God does not favor divorce. Since He never intended for there to be such a thing as divorce, He made no provision for it. We cannot deny that divorce does exist, but from the beginning it was not so. Divorce is not God's invention—it is man's. (Matt. 19:7,8.)

Divorce Hurts God

I don't believe we have begun to comprehend how much God is hurt by the things that cause us pain. The reason I'm convinced of that is because of the number of Christians today who believe that it is God who is bringing hurtful things upon His children. They believe that somehow God uses these things to teach us lessons, to keep us humble or obedient or dependent upon Him, or to draw us closer to Him.

But once we realize that every time we are hurt, God Himself hurts, we begin to view God and His will in a different light. No longer do we see the Lord as a jealous monarch whose purpose it is to keep His subjects in humble submission to Him, but rather He becomes a loving heavenly Father who delights in giving the kingdom to His own children. (Luke 12:32.)

It is not God who puts cancer on people, who causes them to go bankrupt, who maims and kills innocent children, who wrecks homes and robs husbands and wives of their mates and children of their parents. It is not God who comes to steal, and to kill, and to destroy. (John 10:10.)

Until the Church learns to distinguish between the works of God and the works of the enemy, Satan will continue to wreak havoc on God's children and lay the blame for it all on Him! If anything hurts God, it is to see His own dear children suffer. But the cruelest cut of all must be when they then attribute that suffering to the will of their loving Father!

It is not God's will for His children to hurt, any more than it is our will for our children to hurt. He hurts with us, as we hurt with our offspring.

When I defined sin earlier, I said that in the Old Testament it was an act. A person had to do something to sin, and then he had to do something to correct it. But in the New Testament we see that sin is a selfish decision that hurts God. All that is necessary for the forgiveness of sin is the decision to repent of the sin and to ask for pardon.

Every divorce is the result of a selfish decision that hurts God. **Every** divorce.

By that do I mean that no one should ever get a divorce? No, I didn't say that. What I said was that every divorce is a *result* of someone's selfish decision that hurts God.

Divorce Is Selfish

Let me give you an example. A young woman in her late twenties, single, never married—a lovely young Christian lady who loved God with all her heart—took a trip to another state. There she met a man. They became acquainted and began to date. In a short while they decided to get married. Everybody thought it was wonderful. The two seemed to be so ideally suited for each other.

In spite of how right everything seemed to be, the young woman's pastor was concerned. Did anyone really know anything about the man? Was the young lady absolutely sure who it was she was pledging herself to for life? So he counseled with the young lady.

"Before I perform this ceremony," he told her, "I would like to check this man out a little, find out something about his family and background."

"No, no," the young woman insisted. "I don't want you to do that. It's not necessary. Everything is fine—I just know it is. I love him, and that's all I need to know. I'm going to marry him. If you don't want to marry us, then I'll find someone who will."

So against his better judgment, the pastor reluctantly agreed to perform the ceremony. The couple was united, and sure enough in a few weeks the man began to behave very strangely. He began to disappear for hours at a time. Soon he would be gone all night, with no explanation to his distraught young bride. Finally, the pastor decided to do some investigating on his own. He was shocked to discover that the man had children by his first wife from whom he had never been divorced and who knew nothing of his second marriage. Of course, his new bride had their marriage annulled as soon as possible. In essence, she divorced him.

That divorce was the result of a selfish decision which displeased God. But whose decision? The man's, or the young lady's? Or both? Obviously, the man's decision to commit bigamy was selfish and displeasing to God. That is undeniable. But what about the young woman's decision that despite her pastor's counsel she was going to marry the man without taking the time to learn anything at all about him? Was that decision selfish?

If we could know all the facts of every divorce, we would discover that without exception the primary cause was *selfishness.* Either one or the other or both of the parties involved in a divorce is acting out of self-ishness to one degree or the other. Does that mean that we are to lay blame on one or the other or both? No. I am not talking about who is to blame for any one particular divorce; I am simply pointing out the root cause of divorce itself.

Divorce is the end result of selfish decisions which displease and hurt God. Whenever any couple is involved in a divorce, the first thing most people want to do is to fix the blame. That may be natural, but it's not scriptural. As Christians, fixing the blame is not our job. Our duty and responsibility is to find the cure. And the best cure for any disease has always been *prevention.*

Take Heed to Your Spirit

Malachi 2:15 tells us: **...therefore take heed to your spirit.** We have seen that that spirit is not the husband's spirit or the wife's spirit, but is their new spirit of oneness together. If the marriage partners are each taking heed to that spirit of oneness, they will not allow anything to happen that will destroy their relationship with each other, their spiritual unity.

It is so much better to stop divorce before it ever gets started. If you and your mate are involved in a strained relationship right now, if you are separated, you know in your heart if it was your selfish decision that started the whole thing. You know. If you don't know for sure, then stop and ask yourself, was it *my* selfishness that caused this relationship to disintegrate?

Ask God about it. He will reveal the truth of the matter to you. After all, God is more concerned about that selfish decision than He is about the fact that you and your mate may no longer be physically living together at the moment. He knows that until you become one in spirit, sharing the same house won't make any real difference.

There are many estranged married people who think they would please God if they could just get their mate to come back home. That is not necessarily so. In my years of counseling, there have been many people who have told me, "Oh, if I could just get my mate to come back home, I would be happy. All I want is for our children to have their mother and father together again."

Unless the issue dividing two marriage partners is settled, there is no more of a home with them together than there is with them apart. Physical separation is only symptomatic—the real problem is spiritual. That's why God is more concerned about the selfishness of the partners than He is about whether or not they are living under the same roof.

If that is your situation right now, you need to become more concerned with your spirit of oneness with your mate than you are with his or her place of residence! If you get your spirit of unity restored, everything else will fall into place. If you don't restore (or establish) that unity, no amount of living together will make a marriage. If your marriage has fallen apart, if you made the selfish decision that brought about the divorce or separation, ask God to forgive you. If you do that, God will forgive you. Accept that forgiveness and go on with your life.

But what if you are separated or divorced and the selfish decision was not yours, but your mate's? What can you do then? Pray for your mate just as you would for yourself. Forgive him or her and ask God to do the same. Continue to hold your mate up before the Lord in prayer, blessing him or her with love, joy, wisdom and peace, always thinking and speaking well of them. Hold fast to your confession, confident that true to His promise God will work all things for good to those who love Him and who are fitting in with His plans. (Rom. 8:28.)

God Forgives Divorce

Did you know that everyone who has ever asked God to forgive them of making a selfish decision that was displeasing to Him has been forgiven? The Apostle John has assured us, **If we confess our sins, he** (God) **is faithful and just to forgive us our sins, and to cleanse us from all unrighteousness** (1 John 1:9).

But did you also know that God has actually forgiven us *before* we even ask? In 2 Corinthians 5:19 Paul writes: "It was God (personally present) in Christ, reconciling and restoring the world to favor with Himself, *not counting up and holding against [men] their trespasses [but cancelling them];* and committing to us the message of reconciliation—of the restoration to favor" (AMP).

Notice that this is past tense. In Christ, God has already forgiven and canceled our sins. The forgiveness is already there, knocking on our door, pressuring us to receive it. That's right. You don't have to beg God to forgive you. If anything, He's pleading with you to accept His forgiveness. You don't have to talk God into granting you pardon. He's trying to talk you into receiving what He has already done for you in His Son Jesus Christ. That's why He is having me write these things.

There are people who have asked God to forgive them, but who have never accepted the fact that He has done what they requested Him to do. Some people tell me, "I have asked God to forgive me."

"Well then," I answer, "He has done it."

"Oh, but I don't feel like I'm forgiven," they say. "I don't feel any different."

Forgiveness isn't received by feelings, it is received by faith. I've encountered a lot of people who have a hard time accepting forgiveness. They think that in order to be forgiven they have to *do* something. They feel they somehow have to try to set things right, to make restitution.

A friend of mine and his wife were living very carnal lives. As a result, she met another man and eventually moved in with him. A few years later, she and my friend were divorced. Later on, my friend mentioned to me that he had talked with his mother about the situation.

"Son, you are living in sin," she told him. "Unless you can get your ex-wife to get a divorce and come back and marry you, you will die and go to hell."

Can you believe that? And this is a highly respected woman, a so-called teacher of the Word. Dear God, that's not the Word! That's about as far from the Word of God as a person can get. In the first place, God doesn't send anybody to hell for being divorced. And secondly, even if the man was to blame, all he had to do to be forgiven was to ask. He didn't have to get his wife back before he could be pardoned. That idea is ridiculous. Yet many people actually believe that they have to get their broken marriage back together or else they can't be forgiven. That just isn't so.

Suppose a man is divorced and his former wife has remarried. Did you know that there are some people who are so misguided they would advise that man, "Well, since both you and your ex-wife are Christians, you ought to pray that her new husband will either divorce her or die so she can come back and remarry you"! Is that Christian?

How unscriptural can people get? Why do they believe and teach such nonsense? Where do such outlandish ideas come from? Part of the problem is the false notion that forgiveness is conditioned upon restoration or restitution. People mistakenly think that God cannot or will not forgive unless "things are set right."

If you are divorced or separated, of course you should get your marriage restored if you can. If it is at all possible to reconcile your relationship, then do so. That goal ought to be foremost in your mind. But sometimes marriages just can't be put back together. Many people do "reconcile" their relationship. They get back together. But because they don't resolve the spiritual situation that caused the problem in the first place, soon the marriage falls apart again. And it will continue to do so until that spiritual union is established. Without it, there really is no marriage to reconcile.

What I am saying is simply this: You can straighten out your part of the spiritual problem whether you ever get your marriage together or not. Before God, you are an individual. You stand alone before Him, just you. Whether you are ever able to get your marriage straightened out or not, whether you can reconcile it again or not, has nothing to do with whether or not you can be forgiven.

You see, you don't "unsteal" something to be forgiven of stealing. Of course, you take the stolen item back if you can. But you cannot "unsteal." Neither can you "unlie." If you tell a lie, you have told a lie. You can't "unlie." You just have to admit that your statement was untrue and ask forgiveness for lying.

Suppose you were to kill someone. Would you have to raise that person from the dead before you could be forgiven? If so, there wouldn't be much hope for you, would there? How could any unforgiven person raise the dead? That would be difficult enough for someone who is in right relationship and fellowship with God. How could a non-forgiven person possibly raise someone from the dead in order to be forgiven? How can you "uncriticize" someone? "Unhurt" someone? You can't. But you can be forgiven of hurting, criticizing, killing, lying, stealing—or divorcing.

If divorce causes a person to be guilty of adultery, how can he be freed of that sin unless he can get his marriage back together? By now the answer ought to be obvious. He can receive forgiveness.

You'll notice that I said *receive* forgiveness. There have been people who have sat in my office, looked me straight in the eye and said, "I am divorced, and I know I can never be forgiven. I'm living in sin, but I can't help it. My former mate is married again and now has a wonderful relationship with someone else. So that leaves me in a state of adultery. Since I can't get my marriage back together, there is no way for me to be forgiven." Do you see the ignorance of that statement? Do you see how it contradicts the Word of God?

I want you to know, there is only one thing that is unpardonable. That is the refusal to receive pardon. The only sin God cannot forgive is the sin of rejection of His forgiveness. If He says, "I forgive you," and a person answers, "I don't believe it, I don't accept it," then that person is unpardonable. The thing that makes the unpardonable sin unpardonable is the fact that the person will not receive pardon. Will not. And if a person will not, God cannot. That's true.

There is no wrong so great that the blood of Jesus does not cover it, no sin so vile that God can't forgive it. The only possible way for a sin to be unforgivable is for the person who committed it to say no to the forgiveness which God offers. Yet we've looked at this whole issue of marriage, divorce and adultery and have built a case that it is something too big for God to handle. We have said that unless we in our little frail human bodies can do something physical to rectify our situation, then God's hands are tied. How many people have we destined to "live in sin" because we have based forgiveness on their action rather than on the grace and mercy of Almighty God?

God can and does forgive divorce. Sin is a selfish decision that displeases God. If you have made such a decision in regard to your marriage, in regard to divorce, in regard to remarriage, whether it's the first time or the fiftieth time, God can and will forgive you.

If your marriage is broken and you have the opportunity to get it back together, then by all means do so. I believe you ought to do everything in your power to be reconciled to your mate. I am not advocating divorce, or remarriage, anymore than I am advocating adultery. Nor am I in any way opposed to reconciliation. I believe in reconciliation. But the truth is, there are some situations in which reconciliation is just not possible, as for example where one of the divorced parties has already remarried. In a case like that, to whom can the single mate be reconciled? You can't unscramble eggs. Sometimes, sad to say, the best that can be done is to forget the past and begin anew. As Christians we ought to be sensitive and caring enough to allow divorced people a chance at a new beginning, free from slander, gossip, guilt and judgment.

Beloved, if God so loved us, we ought also to love one another, wrote John, the apostle of love. (1 John 4:11.) If God forgives divorce, if He loves and pardons divorced people, who are we to judge or condemn?

3

Is Divorce Adultery?

When a man hath taken a wife, and married her,
and it come to pass that she find no favour in his eyes,
because he hath found some uncleanness in her: then
let him write her a bill of divorcement, and give it
in her hand, and send her out of his house.

And when she is departed out of his house, she
may go and be another man's wife.

And if the latter husband hate her, and write her
a bill of divorcement, and giveth it in her hand, and
sendeth her out of his house; or if the latter husband
die, which took her to be his wife;

Her former husband, which sent her away, may
not take her again to be his wife, after that she is
defiled; for that is abomination before the Lord: and
thou shalt not cause the land to sin, which the Lord
thy God giveth thee for an inheritance.

Deuteronomy 24:1-4

In his book, *Manners and Customs of Bible Lands,*
Mr. Fred H. Wight records these words:

"For centuries it has been possible for a husband
in Arab lands to divorce his wife by a spoken word.
The wife thus divorced is entitled to all her wearing
apparel, and the husband cannot take from her anything she has upon her own person. For this reason,
coins on the head gear, and rings and necklaces,
become important wealth in the hour of the divorced
woman's great need. This is one reason why there is
so much interest in the bride's personal adornment in
Eastern countries. Such customs of divorce were no
doubt prevalent in Gentile lands in Old Testament

times. It was for this reason that the Law of Moses limited the power of the husband to divorce his wife by requiring that he must give her a written bill of divorcement. (Deut. 24:1.) Thus the Jewish custom of divorce was superior to the Arabic.''[1]

Based on this evidence, it becomes clear that the Mosaic Law was not given to make divorce easier, but in fact to make it more difficult. Contrary to the usual custom of that time and area, the Hebrew male could not, as most Arabs, divorce his wife by a simple spoken word, but had to provide her with a written bill of divorcement. Actual copies of this document can be found in various Bible commentaries and reference books.

This law was initiated by Moses for the benefit and protection of the Jewish wives. Considering the low estate of women in that early male-dominated society, it is likely that many Jewish wives would have been in real danger of their lives had Moses not issued this decree. If the law had simply forbidden the Jewish men to remarry except at the death of their wives, due to the "hardness of their hearts" at least some of those men might have found it expedient to see that their wives "passed on" before their time.

In Matthew 19:8 Jesus explains to the Jews that this law had been given to them by Moses because of the hardness of their hearts, but points out that "from the beginning it was not so." Meaning, of course, that such a system was never God's intention or plan.

We must keep in mind that what Jesus had to say about marriage, divorce and adultery in the nineteenth

---

[1]*Manners and Customs of Bible Lands* (Chicago: Moody Press, 1953), p. 125.

chapter of Matthew was directed to the Jews of His day and dealt with their misconceptions of these things. What He had to say must be interpreted in the light of that context.

The Jewish Law on Divorce

With that understanding then, let's go back and look at Deuteronomy 24 in closer detail.

When a man hath taken a wife, and married her, and it come to pass that she find no favour in his eyes, because he hath found some uncleanness in her.... I believe what Moses meant here was simply, ''If a man marries a woman and then finds out that she is not a virgin....'' But it is pretty obvious that when Jesus was confronted with the questions of the Jews about marriage and divorce, they had come to the point of taking the ''uncleanness'' of Deuteronomy 24:1 to mean anything about a wife that displeased her husband.

Thus in Jesus' day, a Jewish man could divorce his wife for virtually any reason. That's what prompted the question put to Him by the Pharisees in Matthew 19:3: **Is it lawful for a man to put away his wife for** *every* **cause?** And we know that Jesus' reply was, in essence, ''No, when God unites a man and a woman in matrimony, He never intends for that union to be dissolved.''

''Well, then,'' counter the Pharisees, ''if that's so, why did Moses command that a bill of divorcement be given the wife by the husband?''

"Because he knew the hard-heartedness of the Jewish males," Jesus responds. "But although Moses allowed a bill of divorcement for the protection of the subservient and dependent wives, divorce was never God's idea."

(It might be pointed out here that to the Jew, divorce was totally a man's perogative. Nothing was said about a woman's marrying a man and then finding some fault in him, which is not at all surprising in view of the Jewish society of that day.)

And when she is departed out of his house, she may go and be another man's wife. Now please take note: Nothing—absolutely nothing—is mentioned here about adultery. Yet it is obvious that the man who sent his wife away had every intention of taking another wife. And he was in no way forbidden to do so.

And if the latter husband hate her, and write her a bill of divorcement, and giveth it in her hand, and sendeth her out of his house; or if the latter husband die, which took her to be his wife, her former husband, which sent her away, may not take her again to be his wife, after that she is defiled.... So according to Mosaic law, it was forbidden for a man to remarry his former wife if she had ever been the wife of another man. Why? Because she was considered "defiled."

What does it mean to be defiled? That is perhaps the strongest expression in the whole statement. We understand that to mean that in terms of the *ceremonial* law, the woman was unclean, she was contaminated. Well, let me ask you a question. Does this Jewish law relate to us today? As Christians, are you and I bound by Jewish ceremonial law? Thank God, no. Then if that is the case, would it not be safe to say that all the Old Covenant laws and customs need to be subjected to and interpreted in the light of the New Covenant?

Even under the ceremonial law remarriage was no problem either to the man or the woman as long as the man did not take back his former wife who had been remarried, or as long as the woman did not marry a Levite, a member of the priestly order. If either of these two things did take place, it was plainly labeled an abomination before the Lord. An abomination is a divine abhorrence. The woman was free to marry any other man without penalty, and her former husband was free to marry any other woman.

Then why are there preachers today who counsel divorced people whose former mate has remarried to believe God that the second mate will get a divorce or die so the original partners can get back together? The Bible plainly states that such a remarriage is an abomination before the Lord. In view of this conflict, it seems obvious that we need to give careful consideration to the passages in both the Old and New Testaments before making any sweeping judgments about these crucial matters of divorce, remarriage and adultery.

Jesus' Words on Divorce

Jesus was more knowledgeable about these things than you and I. He understood this whole situation completely. Before we go any further, I think we should stop to collect our thoughts for a moment and see what was in the mind and heart of Jesus when He made the statements we are about to consider in the fifth and nineteenth chapters of Matthew and the tenth chapter of Mark.

The first thing we need to note is that Jesus knew the past hardness of the hearts of the people to whom He was speaking these words.

The second thing we should be aware of is that Jesus knew the present hardness of the hearts of these people. The Jews at the time of Jesus were no softer of heart than the people of Moses' day—if anything, they were harder. This Jesus knew full well. He knew, too, that the matter of divorce was not what God had intended when He created Adam and Eve. Keep this in mind: *Jesus also knew that adultery had never been associated with divorce in the minds of these people.* That point is very important to a clear understanding of His words to them on this issue.

If you will look throughout the Old Testament, you will not find any connection whatsoever between divorce and adultery, or between remarriage and adultery. Adultery was a capital offense. Anyone found guilty of adultery was stoned to death. Jesus knew that. He also knew that after the resurrection that was about to take place after His crucifixion and burial, men and women were going to be born again. They were going to be made spiritually alive. For the first time since Adam and Eve, for the first time since the fall of man, the relationship between a man and his wife could finally be what God intended it to be. With all of His heart, Jesus wanted to prepare His listeners— including us—for that relationship.

Jesus also wanted these people and us to understand how seriously God views this relationship between a husband and wife. All this was clearly in the heart and mind of Jesus when He was confronted with these people's questions about marriage and divorce.

There are at least three things that Jesus never intended to do in the statements that He made in reply to these questions: 1) He never intended to break the law. 2) He never intended to make it harder to live for God under the New Covenant than it had been under the Old Covenant. 3) He never intended for us to look at anything He said or did, apart from the Law of Love.

In the statements we are about to read and consider, Jesus is simply confirming that divorce is wrong, that divorce is a sin. But you will see right away that He is also adding a new dimension to divorce, and that is the dimension of adultery.

> Ye have heard that it was said by them of old time, Thou shalt not commit adultery:
>
> But I say unto you, That whosoever looketh on a woman to lust after her hath committed adultery with her already in his heart.
>
> And if thy right eye offend thee, pluck it out, and cast it from thee: for it is profitable for thee that one of thy members should perish, and not that thy whole body should be cast into hell.
>
> And if thy right hand offend thee, cut it off, and cast it from thee: for it is profitable for thee that one of thy members should perish, and not that thy whole body should be cast into hell.
>
> It hath been said, Whosoever shall put away his wife, let him give her a writing of divorcement:
>
> But I say unto you, That whosoever shall put away his wife, saving for the cause of fornication, causeth her to commit adultery: and whosoever shall marry her that is divorced committeth adultery.
>
> **Matthew 5:27-32**

And it came to pass, that when Jesus had finished these sayings, he departed from Galilee, and came into the coasts of Judaea beyond Jordan.

And great multitudes followed him; and he healed them there.

The Pharisees also came unto him, tempting him, and saying unto him, Is it lawful for a man to put away his wife for every cause?

And he answered and said unto them, Have ye not read, that he which made them at the beginning made them male and female.

And said, For this cause shall a man leave father and mother, and shall cleave to his wife: and they twain shall be one flesh?

Wherefore they are no more twain, but one flesh. What therefore God hath joined together, let not man put asunder.

They say unto him, Why did Moses then command to give a writing of divorcement, and to put her away?

He saith unto them, Moses because of the hardness of your hearts, suffered you to put away your wives: but from the beginning it was not so.

And I say unto you, Whosoever shall put away his wife, except it be for fornication, and shall marry another, committeth adultery: and whoso marry her which is put away doth commit adultery.

Matthew 19:1-9

A New Connection

I can find absolutely no record in the Old Covenant that makes the connection between adultery and divorce, or adultery and remarriage, that we find in these two passages. According to Leviticus 20:10 and Deuteronomy 22:22, anyone who was guilty of adultery was to be killed. Consider the impact of Jesus' words here on the Jewish people who have questioned Him about divorce. Put yourself in their place for a moment.

Suppose you were a Jewish male, well versed in the Mosaic Law, knowing full well the penalty for adultery. If you heard Jesus say that putting away your wife except for the cause of fornication made you guilty of adultery, how would you react? Especially if you had already divorced your wife?

Jesus makes a startling connection between divorce and adultery. And between remarriage and adultery. As a Jewish male you would have thought, *Does Jesus have in mind the very same thing that we find in the Law? Does Jesus mean that when people divorce they are guilty of adultery in the same way that Leviticus 20 and Deuteronomy 22 speak of adultery? If so, are we to stone them to death?* Stoning was the common form of capital punishment in those days. Remember that according to the Law, adultery was a capital offense.

Is that what Jesus meant? Of course not. You and I know that. Yet we have stoned a lot of people with our words.

Adultery Defined

Jesus went unto the mount of Olives.

And early in the morning he came again into the temple, and all the people came unto him; and he sat down, and taught them.

And the scribes and Pharisees brought unto him a woman taken in adultery; and when they had set her in the midst,

They say unto him, Master, this woman was taken in adultery, in the very act.

> Now Moses in the law commanded us, that such should be stoned: but what sayest thou?
>
> This they said, tempting him, that they might have to accuse him. But Jesus stooped down, and with his finger wrote on the ground, as though he heard them not.
>
> So when they continued asking him he lifted up himself, and said unto them, He that is without sin among you, let him first cast a stone at her.
>
> And again he stooped down and wrote on the ground.
>
> And they which heard it, being convicted by their own conscience, went out one by one, beginning at the eldest, even unto the last: and Jesus was left alone, and the woman standing in the midst.
>
> When Jesus had lifted up himself, and saw none but the woman, he said unto her, Woman, where are those thine accusers? hath no man condemned thee?
>
> She said, No man, Lord. And Jesus said unto her, Neither do I condemn thee: go, and sin no more.
>
> **John 8:1-11**

According to the way many people have treated the subject of divorce and remarriage, after everybody else had left, Jesus should have stoned the woman Himself. But He didn't. That should give us some idea as to God's view of this whole subject.

Webster's Dictionary defines adultery as: "**1.** Violation of the marriage bed; sexual intercourse between a married man and a woman not his wife, or between a married woman and a man not her husband. *Adultery* is a common legal ground for divorce. **2.** In Scripture, all manner of lewdness or unchastity; also, idolatry or apostasy."[2]

---

[2]*Webster's New Twentieth Century Dictionary of the English Language Unabridged,* 2nd ed., s.v. "adultery."

This woman was obviously sexually involved with a man who was not her husband. She had been caught in the very act. There was no question of her guilt.

Is it possible that these scribes and Pharisees were some of the ones who had heard Jesus make the statements that we read in Matthew 19? Could it be that they had heard Him say the things we see recorded in Matthew 5 about divorce and adultery, and so they decided that the best way to test what He meant was to find someone they knew was involved in adultery—sexual adultery—someone they could prove was guilty of adultery under the Law—and then take that person to Jesus to see what He would do with her?

Do you see the trap they were laying for Jesus? The Law said that such a person was to be stoned to death. If Jesus agreed with the Law, then what about His message of love and forgiveness? But if He said not to stone her, He would appear to be breaking the Law of Moses. But notice, this is a double trap.

Based on the statements He had made about divorce and remarriage, if Jesus said to stone the woman, He would be admitting that all those who have divorced or remarried should similarly be stoned to death for adultery. If He said not to stone her, He would seem to be implying that adultery is excusable. Either way, He seemed to be trapped. But of course He was far too wise to fall for the Pharisees' deception. By turning the issue back on them, He avoided having to take either alternative.

The issue involved here is much deeper than the Jews and the Pharisees realized. What Jesus was actually doing by His statements was redefining adultery. He was, in essence, adding the second definition.

Adultery is a sin. Everybody knows that. Sexual involvement between a married person and someone other than his or her mate is a sin. That is undeniable. But Jesus even expanded and spiritualized this first and physical definition of adultery by noting that the act itself was not necessary, that mere inward lustful desire was enough to constitute adultery.

But if we are talking about the true spiritual definition of adultery, then we are referring to idolatry or apostasy.

In either case, whether physical or spiritual, adultery is a sin. In John 8:11 Jesus said to the woman, **...go, and *sin* no more.** But the good news to the repentant heart is that adultery can be forgiven. The New Covenant does not do away with the sin of adultery, but it does provide for pardon for the one guilty of it. That is the point that needs to be emphasized by us Christians. More than the existence and penalty of sin, we need to learn to stress forgiveness of sin.

What Is Adultery?

Then cometh he to a city of Samaria, which is called Sychar, near to the parcel of ground that Jacob gave to his son Joseph.

Now Jacob's well was there. Jesus therefore, being wearied with his journey, sat thus on the well: and it was about the sixth hour.

There cometh a woman of Samaria to draw water: Jesus saith unto her, Give me to drink.

(For his disciples were gone away unto the city to buy meat.)

Then saith the woman of Samaria unto him, How is it that thou, being a Jew, askest drink of me, which am a woman of Samaria? for the Jews have no dealings with the Samaritans.

Jesus answered and said unto her, If thou knewest the gift of God, and who it is that saith to thee, Give me to drink; thou wouldest have asked of him, and he would have given thee living water.

The woman saith unto him, Sir, thou hast nothing to draw with, and the well is deep: from whence then hast thou that living water?

Art thou greater than our father Jacob, which gave us the well, and drank thereof himself, and his children, and his cattle?

Jesus answered and said unto her, Whosoever drinketh of this water shall thirst again:

But whosoever drinketh of the water that I shall give him shall never thirst; but the water that I shall give him shall be in him a well of water springing up into everlasting life.

The woman saith unto him, Sir, give me this water, that I thirst not, neither come hither to draw.

Jesus saith unto her, Go, call thy husband, and come hither.

The woman answered and said, I have no husband.

Jesus said unto her, Thou hast well said, I have no husband:

For thou has had five husbands; and he whom thou hast now is not thy husband: in that saidst thou truly.

The woman said unto him, Sir, I perceive that thou art a prophet.

Our fathers worshipped in this mountain; and ye say, that in Jerusalem is the place where men ought to worship.

Jesus saith unto her, Woman, believe me, the hour cometh, when ye shall neither in this mountain, nor yet at Jerusalem, worship the Father.

Ye worship ye know not what: we know what we worship: for salvation is of the Jews.

But the hour cometh, and now is, when the true worshippers shall worship the Father in spirit and in truth: for the Father seeketh such to worship him.

God is a Spirit: and they that worship him must worship him in spirit and in truth.

The woman saith unto him, I know that Messias cometh, which is called Christ: when he is come, he will tell us all things.

Jesus saith unto her, I that speak unto thee am he.

And upon this came his disciples, and marvelled that he talked with the woman: yet no man said, What seekest thou? or, Why talkest thou with her?

The woman then left her waterpot, and went her way into the city, and saith to the men,

Come, see a man which told me all things that ever I did: is not this the Christ?

Then they went out of the city, and came unto him.

John 4:5-30

There are those who teach that once a person marries, even if he later gets a legal divorce, even if he marries someone else, he is forever married to his first wife. Yet Jesus did not tell this woman who had been married five times and who was living with a man to whom she was not married, ''You have had one husband and five lovers.'' He said, ''You are right when you say you have no husband: you have had *five* husbands.'' Obviously Jesus thought a person could be married more than once in a lifetime.

64

This story and the one in the eighth chapter of John make it clear that Jesus was not just establishing another law. If Jesus had been establishing another law against adultery by His words in Matthew 19, Matthew 5, and Mark 10, then He should have acted like it. When He encountered this woman who had had five husbands and was now living with a man to whom she was not married. By law He should have stoned her to death. But He didn't. He didn't even condemn her verbally.

Jesus was not replacing one law with another when He made His statements about divorce, remarriage and adultery. Matthew 19 is not a law. Matthew 5 is not a law. Mark 10, which we will look at in the next chapter, is not a law. (In that chapter I will show you from Matthew 19 itself where it clearly states that it is not a law.) Jesus did not come to earth to establish laws or to do away with laws; He came to fulfill the law. (Matt. 5:17.)

Then what was Jesus saying when He talked about divorce and remarriage? Simply stated, He was saying that there is more than one definition of adultery. The Jews defined adultery as immoral sex, a violation of Jewish Law punishable by death. In the eighth chapter of John, where the woman caught in adultery was brought to Jesus, He agrees with the Jews that immoral sex is adultery. But He also makes it clear that the person guilty of adultery is *not* to be condemned: **He that is without sin among you, let him first cast a stone...**(v. 7).

There are many people today who still define adultery only as immoral sex. To them any union between a man and a woman who are not the first

husband and first wife is immoral. The only exception is the case of a widow or widower who may remarry without penalty, provided he or she remarries someone who has never been married or whose first mate has died. According to this definition, every remarried person whose mate did not leave him or her widowed, is guilty of adultery. I have even heard people say, "It's all right for a divorced person to remarry—as long as they don't have sex. That would be adultery!" How we have twisted the Scriptures!

According to *Strong's Concordance*, the Hebrew word most often used and translated in English as "adultery" is *na aph*, which means: "to *commit adultery;* fig. to *apostatize:* —adulterer(-ess), commit(-ing) adultery, woman that breaketh wedlock."[3] In his *Hebrew—Chaldee Lexicon To The Old Testament*, Dr. William Gesenius defines this same Hebrew word: "to commit adultery, used both of the male and female...to commit adultery with a woman...In the same manner as...[the Hebrew word which means] to commit a fornication, it is applied to the turning aside of Israel from the true God to the worship of idols...."[4] Dr. Gesenius then gives examples.

Now we have three basic definitions of adultery: 1) Immoral sex. 2) A woman breaking wedlock. 3) Apostasy, which means to fall away from God, to break fellowship with God, to abandon one's faith or belief, or literally "to stand away from in varying degrees."

---

[3]*Strong's*, p. 75 of Heb. and Chald. Dictionary.

[4]*Lexicon Manuale Hebraicum et Chaldaicum in Veteris Testamenti Libros*, trans. Samuel Prideaux Tragelles (Grand Rapids: Baker Book House, 1979), p. 525.

In Matthew 5:32 Jesus said, **...I say unto you, That whosoever shall put away** (divorce) **his wife, saving for the cause of fornication, causeth her to commit adultery** (Greek, *moichao*)**: and whosoever shall marry her that is divorced committeth adultery** (*moichao*). This Greek word *moichao* translated "adultery" has basically the same meaning as the Hebrew word *na aph*. In fact, all the Greek words used in the New Testament relating to adultery are from the same root word which can be translated either as *adultery* or as *apostasy*.

Which of these two meanings did Jesus have in mind here in Matthew 5:32? Was He referring literally to adultery (immoral sex), or figuratively to apostasy (falling away from or breaking fellowship with God)?

In Matthew 19:9 Jesus repeated this statement: **Whosoever shall put away his wife, except it be for fornication, and shall marry another, committeth...***moichao*: **and whoso marrieth her which is put away doth commit...***moichao*. These are the same basic Greek words meaning adultery or apostasy. Which is it?

If a woman was put away because she had committed fornication, then she would have already fallen away from God. She broke fellowship with Him the moment she committed fornication. But if a man divorced his wife who had not committed fornication, then it was he who was guilty of adultery by causing her to commit apostasy, along with anyone else who subsequently married her.

Of course, apostasy is only one of three possible definitions of adultery. But what I am pointing out is that in every case where that Hebrew or Greek word is used in the Scriptures, we need to examine the context carefully to determine just which definition to apply. With three possibilities, how can we be absolutely sure which one is correct? Someone had to make the decision to put the word adultery in the English translation of these Scriptures upon which we are judging not only divorce but divorced people.

It is entirely possible that Matthew 5:32, for example, might be properly translated: "Whoever puts away his wife, except for the cause of fornication, causes her to commit *apostasy*: and whoever marries her that is put away commits *apostasy*." That would put a whole new light on the subject, wouldn't it? It might also explain some obvious misunderstandings and misinterpretations of Jesus' words and attitude toward divorce, remarriage and adultery.

Joseph H. Thayer, in his *A Greek-English Lexicon of the New Testament*, gives even more detailed information on these Greek words translated "adultery," bearing out the fact of two possible interpretations or translations of them.[5] Noted Bible scholar W. E. Vine also supports this view.[6] Based on this information, it seems safe to say that no one can use these particular Bible passages as a concrete basis for the doctrine that any divorced person who remarries is "living in adultery."

---

[5]*Grimm's Wilke's Clavis Novi Testamenti*, 4th ed., trans. Joseph Henry Thayer (Nashville: Broadman Press, 1977. Reprinted by permission of Baker Book House.) p. 417.

[6]W. E. Vine, *An Expository Dictionary of New Testament Words* (Old Tappan: Revell, 1966), vol. I, pp. 32,33.

Have you ever heard that expression used in reference to a divorced person who has remarried someone other than his or her original mate? Did you know that one reason why many people believe God can't forgive them is because they have been told repeatedly that they are "living in adultery," "living in sin"?

Did you also know that there are many born-again, Spirit-filled Christians, people who love God with all their hearts, who earnestly believe because they are divorced and remarried that every time they have sex they have to ask God to forgive them of committing adultery? Why? Because of the teaching of this false doctrine. Yes, I said false. It is false because it simply cannot be substantiated by the original language of the Bible texts on which it is supposedly based.

In a matter this serious, this far-reaching, we must be careful to study the context of the statements on which we build our doctrines. We must also remember to interpret those statements in light of the love and forgiveness of a merciful God **Who also hath made us able ministers of the new testament; not of the** *letter***, but of the** *spirit***: for the letter killeth, but the spirit giveth life** (2 Cor. 3:6), **and where the Spirit of the Lord is, there is liberty** (2 Cor. 3:17).

So to the usual Jewish definitions of adultery Jesus added these: 1) The decision to lust, and 2) apostasy caused by being put away from one's mate. Does that mean that when a person puts away his or her mate, the putting away causes the mate to become sexually immoral? Is that what Jesus meant? How could that be if he or she never again has a sexual relationship? Evidently Jesus' second definition of adultery is quite different from His first. In that case, is divorce adultery? Perhaps a better way to phrase that question would be, is divorce *necessarily* adultery?

4

Is Remarriage Immoral?

Ye have heard it said by them of old time, Thou shalt not commit adultery:

But I say unto you, That whosoever looketh upon a woman to lust after her hath committed adultery with her already in his heart.

And if thy right eye offend thee, pluck it out, and cast it from thee: for it is profitable for thee that one of thy members should perish, and not that thy whole body should be cast into hell.

And if thy right hand offend thee, cut it off, and cast it from thee: for it is profitable for thee that one of thy members should perish, and not that thy whole body should be cast into hell.

It hath been said, Whosoever shall put away his wife, let him give her a writing of divorcement:

But I say unto you, That whosoever shall put away his wife, saving for the cause of fornication, causeth her to commit adultery: and whosoever shall marry her that is divorced committeth adultery.

Matthew 5:27-32

Any time Jesus or any of the New Testament writers quoted from the Old Testament for the purpose of demonstrating that the New Covenant agrees with or is a fulfillment of the Old, they always quoted verbatim. For example, in Matthew 8:16 when Matthew wrote that Jesus **healed all that were sick**, he adds in verse 17, **That it might be fulfilled which was spoken by Esaias the prophet, saying, Himself took our infirmities, and bare our sicknesses.** To substantiate his case that Jesus was the promised Messiah in fulfillment of Jewish prophecy, Matthew repeatedly quoted Old Testament writers who foretold of the coming Christ and His words and deeds.

But notice how Jesus quoted the Old Testament here in this passage: **Ye have** *heard it said* **by them of old time, Thou shalt not commit adultery.** Then He added, **But** *I* **say unto you....** There is a difference between the way Jesus phrased this commandment and the way things are usually quoted in the New Testament. He added something before and after the quote. Before the quote He added the phrase, **Ye have heard it said by them of old time**. After the quote He added the phrase, **But I say unto you**. Why? Jesus worded this statement this way because He was about to say something that sounded very different from the commandment, ''Thou shalt not commit adultery.'' And, as we have already seen, what He said different was that adultery (like all sin) is not just an act, as these people had always been taught, but was in fact a decision.

In His statement in Matthew 5 we have said that Jesus was making a distinction between an act and a decision: ''You heard it was said, 'Don't commit adultery,' but I say, 'Don't even look to lust.' '' We have also seen that Jesus then went on to expound on this new definition of adultery by teaching the people, **If thy right eye offend thee, pluck it out** (v. 29).

What about the left eye? How can a person's right eye offend him and not his left? Don't people look with both eyes? Was Jesus speaking literally of plucking out eyeballs? In His public ministry Jesus restored sight to many blind people. Was the one Who healed so many blind eyes actually saying for us to pull our eyeballs out of our head? If not, then what was He saying?

In verse 30 of this same passage Jesus added: **And if thy right hand offend thee, cut it off....** Is this not the same Jesus who healed a man of a withered hand? (Matt. 12:10-13.) Did He really intend for us to literally chop off our hands? Was He foolish enough to think we could stop sin by getting rid of the offending member?

No, Jesus knew that sin didn't issue from the eye anymore than it did from the hand. Then why did He make such bizarre statements? To show forcibly and graphically that the definition of sin had changed from act to decision. Our Lord was not commanding us to mutilate our body. He was teaching us to take command over the members of our body, to bring them into submission to our mind and spirit. Later on, this same idea was expressed by the Apostle Paul in his letters to the Corinthians.

What Jesus was actually saying was, ''If your right eye or hand is causing you to fall for Satan's temptation, make the decision that you will not allow it to do so. Take authority and control over your body, bring it into submission to your will.'' Sin is a decision of the mind, not an act of the body.

Whose Decision Is Divorce?

Is there then any connection between Jesus' remarks in verses 27-32 and His new definition of sin as a decision? I believe there is. Notice verses 31 and 32:

> **It hath been said, Whosoever shall put away his**
> **wife, let him give her a writing of divorcement: But**
> **I say unto you, That whosoever shall put away his**
> **wife, saving for the cause of fornication, causeth her**
> **to commit adultery: and whosoever shall marry her**
> **that is divorced committeth adultery.**

Whose decision was this divorce? The husband's or the wife's? Obviously, it was the husband's decision. Jesus was thus saying, "If a man divorces his wife without proper justification, he *causes her* to commit adultery." Then He added, "And whoever marries her after the divorce commits adultery."

When Jesus used the word adultery, what do you imagine instantly came to the minds of His male Jewish listeners? "Oh, that means I caused my ex-wife, and her new husband, to commit adultery! Is Jesus saying that they must both be stoned to death?"

Let's pause for a moment to reflect on Jesus' comments about adultery. First of all, we remember that adultery does not have to be an act. A person can look to lust and be guilty of adultery. Secondly, since sin is a decision, the one who makes the decision is the one who is guilty before God. Now consider this: If you look at someone to lust after that person, you are the one who has committed adultery, not the person you look at. You are the one who is guilty before God. Because that decision to look was yours.

If the person who makes the decision is the guilty party, then if a man puts away his wife without proper justification, thus causing her to commit adultery, who is responsible for that adultery? Who caused it? The man. It was his decision, and the one who makes the decision is the one who is guilty before God.

So then, we can draw two conclusions from this passage. 1) A person who puts away his mate—because of fornication—is not guilty of adultery. From the context it seems clear that fornication, sexual infidelity, is the only justifiable grounds for divorcing one's mate. 2) A person who puts away his mate, for any reason other than fornication, is guilty of causing that mate (and anyone who marries the one put away) to commit adultery.

Then the question is: In that case, when does adultery take place? In an unjustifiable divorce, at what precise moment does the adultery occur?

When the divorced party remarries?

What if he or she doesn't remarry? Look closely at Matthew 5:32. Jesus didn't say, "Whosoever shall put away his wife, saving for the cause of fornication, causeth her to commit adultery *when she remarries.*" He didn't even imply that. He simply stated that if a man puts away his wife without justifiable reason, he causes her to commit adultery. According to what Jesus said, the woman is guilty of adultery when her husband puts her away. She is guilty even if she never has another sexual relationship in her life, even if she is never involved in the sex act again as long as she lives.

There are people who try to explain this passage by saying that what Jesus meant was that the woman would be caused to commit adultery because now that she doesn't have a sexual mate she will be lusting after every man she sees. But Jesus did not say that if a man divorces his wife without justifiable reason, he causes her to *lust.* He said the man causes her to commit adultery.

Well, what other way could she commit adultery except by lusting after men?

Could it be that Jesus was not speaking of physical, sexual adultery, but was actually referring to *apostasy*?

Divorce as Apostasy

By His remarks could Jesus have meant that when a man puts away his wife without reason, that man disturbs her fellowship with God? Could that tearing apart, that separating of two human spirits, create such a spiritual upheaval that for a time that woman's fellowship with God is broken? Is it possible that the spiritual union between a husband and wife is so profound that to break that oneness disturbs their oneness with their Creator?

From what we have seen about the spiritual significance of marriage, this is more than a mere possibility.

I have never met a divorced person who was not shaken in his or her relationship with God because of the divorce. When divorce occurs, invariably there is a shaking up, a real disturbing of the spirits of the parties involved. Now the end result could be their coming closer to God. That can happen, and does. But rarely without their first experiencing a disturbance in their spirits.

This would explain the reaction of Jesus to the woman taken in adultery and to the woman at the well. In both cases, you will note that He was more concerned about their relationship with the Father than He was about their physical relationship.

Have you ever noticed that in John 8, Jesus never said one word of condemnation to the woman caught in the very act of adultery? He didn't even mention her sinful act nor her partner in it. He simply said, **...go, and sin no more** (v. 11). Obviously He was more concerned about her spiritual relationship with God than her physical relationship with the man involved.

Notice also Jesus' comments to the woman at the well in John 4. Although He called attention to the fact that she had, had five husbands and was now living with a sixth man who was not her lawful husband, Jesus talked with her more about her relationship with Him than He did about her marital (and extramarital) relationships. In fact, when He mentioned her husbands and lover in verses 16-18, the woman quickly changed the subject: **The woman saith unto him, Sir, I perceive that thou art a prophet. Our fathers worshipped in this mountain; and ye say, that in Jerusalem...** (vv. 19,20). Yet Jesus never brought the conversation back around to the subject of her marital indiscretions. He simply forgave her.

That woman became an evangelist and as a result, **...many of the Samaritans of that city believed on him for the saying of the woman....And many more believed because of his own word** (vv. 39,41).

Is Remarriage a Sin?

...and whosoever shall marry her that is divorced committeth adultery (Matt. 5:32). Here Jesus plainly teaches that anyone who marries a divorced person commits adultery. But what kind of adultery? Is He talking about sexual adultery? That's what I was always taught He meant. When we come to these verses of Scripture we tend to forget that adultery can refer to something other than sex. We forget that it has any other meaning.

There are many people who teach that a sexual union between a remarried couple is adulterous. They say that if one of the couple has been divorced, that new sexual relationship is immoral. They also say that if both have been divorced, it's doubly bad—double divorce + double remarriage = double adultery!

Sex in a remarriage has been automatically classified as adultery. But the Bible does not say that remarriage is a sin, that the remarried couple involved in a sexual relationship is living in adultery. In 1 Corinthians 7:1,2 the Apostle Paul writes: **It is good for a man not to touch a woman. Nevertheless, *to avoid fornication*, let *every* man have his own wife, and let *every* woman have her own husband**.

But wasn't Paul talking about the first marriage?

Maybe he was. But if a person has been put away wrongfully, how is he or she supposed to avoid fornication? If sex in a remarriage is automatically wrong, if it is as sinful as sex out of marriage, then why get married? Why remarry at all? Why not just fulfill the sex urge without the necessity or responsibility of marriage?

Notice that Paul doesn't say, ''To avoid fornication, let every man have *just one* wife, and let every woman have *just one* husband.'' What if that first mate should die?

If one purpose of marriage is to provide a lawful fulfillment of the natural sex urge, then why would God deny that very fulfillment to people who have been divorced against their will? He wouldn't. Then what about those whose divorce was not against their will? Are they forever condemned to "live in sin" because of their marriage failure? Would not a loving, forgiving heavenly Father prefer that a victim of divorce, whether it was his fault or not, be allowed to fulfill his natural sex urge with his lawfully married second mate rather than to fulfill it outside of marriage or to "burn" with lust? (1 Cor. 7:9.)

The one thing that is absolutely consistent from the beginning to the end of the Bible is the injunction, "Don't get a divorce, God hates divorce, God hates putting away." Yet there is not one Scripture in the entire Bible that states that God hates remarriage. It can't be found, because it just isn't there.

Whose Guilt Is Divorce?

When a divorce occurs, who is guilty? Who does God hold accountable? So far the evidence seems to be that the one who does the putting away is the guilty party. This does not refer to the one who hires the lawyer or takes the case to court. As we have seen in our discussion of the spiritual union in marriage, the actual putting away occurs months, or even years, before the lawyer is ever called. If the actual putting away occurs before the divorce itself, then when does the adultery occur? When the divorce is granted? When the divorced person remarries? When he or she has sex with the new mate?

The Scriptures we have considered seem to indicate that adultery occurs at the point of divorce. That may be a new concept for you. Most people teach that the adultery doesn't occur until remarriage. That's why they say that it's okay to get a divorce as long as you don't remarry, because if you don't remarry, you don't ever commit adultery. But from what we've seen, the Scriptures seem to indicate that adultery occurs at the time of the putting away.

If Jesus did have in mind the spiritual definition of adultery, which is apostasy or falling away from God, that would have to happen at or before the time of the divorce. When that break comes, the moment of separation between a husband's spirit and the wife's spirit, that's when the adultery—the apostasy—occurs.

Jesus indicated that a divorce is not just a mere legal formality but rather a spiritual rupture or division with deep and far-reaching repercussions. I believe there is such unrest in the spirit of a born-again man or woman who is put away, such upheaval in his or her spirit, that if that individual is aware of the turmoil on the inside and knows how to cope with it, many times the situation can be turned into a spiritual victory. I have seen it happen.

But I also know it can be a very real time of spiritual testing, even spiritual catastrophe, unless that person experiences the acceptance and support of other believers. That's why we as Christians must be very careful about our attitude toward divorce and divorced people, regardless of who may appear to be at fault.

Is It Good to Marry?

In Matthew 19 we have been reading how the Pharisees came to Jesus asking Him questions about marriage and divorce. They wanted to know if it was lawful for a person to divorce his mate.

Perceiving their intentions to try to trap Him into a contradictory statement, the only answer Jesus would give them at that point was to stress the oneness of husband and wife. He refused to discuss all the reasons why a couple could get a divorce. Instead, He emphasized the one reason why they should not be divorced—because God has joined the two together so that they are no longer two but one.

Not satisfied with that answer, the Pharisees pressed the issue by raising the question, **Why did Moses then command to give a writing of divorcement, and to put her** (the wife) **away?** (v. 7).

Notice the duality of that question. "Why did Moses command to give a writing of divorcement? Why did he command to put her away?" Of course, Moses did not command that the wife be put away, he only commanded that a man give her a writing of divorcement *if* he put her away. The Pharisees obviously didn't have a clear understanding of the situation, probably because they were not really seeking to know the truth but to catch Jesus in a misstatement.

In verse 8 Jesus pointed out, **Moses because of the hardness of your hearts suffered you to put away your wives: but from the beginning it was not so.** Note that Jesus corrected the Pharisees here by pointing out that Moses didn't "command" divorce, but rather that he "suffered" (allowed) it because of the hardness of men's hearts. He pointed out that divorce was never God's command or desire.

Then we have seen that Jesus went on to add to this statement an observation about divorce. In verse

9 He stated that any man who puts away his wife without justification causes her (and anyone who marries her) to commit adultery.

Now let's look at verse 10 to see the reaction of Jesus' own disciples to this teaching by their Lord: **His disciples say unto him, If the case of the man be so with his wife, it is not good to marry.**

Do you hear what these men are saying? "Well, if what You say is true, Master, then it would be better for a man not to marry!"

What did they mean by that statement? Being Jewish men themselves and familiar with the Old Testament law on marriage and divorce, these disciples were evidently appalled that their Master would in essence disallow all divorce except in the case of marital infidelity. It seems that God's view of marriage was much stricter than man's, especially in that male-dominated society.

A man had the right and freedom to dispose of his wife at will with no penalty and with no sense of guilt or irresponsibility.

If what Jesus was saying was right, then marriage was no longer a temporary matter of convenience subject to male supremacy.

It was nothing less than a permanent, one-man-one-woman, lifetime contract, as binding on the "superior" male as it was on the "lowly" woman.

Unlike the provisions of Jewish Law, this new interpretation made no allowance for "mistakes" or "second thoughts" on the part of the man. No longer could he freely dismiss his wife at his discretion "for every cause.'' In fact, according to Jesus, there were serious consequences to a man's putting away his wife without justifiable reason. To do so meant that the husband would be responsible for her (and her new mate's) committing adultery, an offense punishable by death. Seemingly, that was a little hard for these tradition-bound Jewish men to swallow—even Jesus' own followers. To them, it seemed that rather than risk liability for the commission of a capital offense, it would be better for a man not to marry at all.

Is Marriage for Everyone?

Let's consider Jesus' response to that reaction: **But he said unto them, All men cannot receive this saying, save they to whom it is given** (v. 11).

First, notice that Jesus did not call this a ''law.'' He said it was a ''saying.'' Laws pertain to everyone, without exception. Yet here Jesus clearly indicated that this ''saying'' was not for everyone (''all men''), but for those ''to whom it is given.'' To whom is it given? To everyone who is married? To every believer?

Let's look at verse 12:

> **For there are some eunuchs, which were so born from their mother's womb: and there are some eunuchs, which were made eunuchs of men: and there be eunuchs, which have made themselves eunuchs for the kingdom of heaven's sake. He that is able to receive it, let him receive it.**

Jesus gave us three classifications of people who can receive this saying. Two of these three are people who are, or have been, rendered physically incapable of sexual relationship, those who have no desire for the opposite sex. Obviously, they would have no trouble receiving the saying. The third group is composed of those who have forsworn marriage and sexual involvement for the sake of the Kingdom of God. Having made such a commitment voluntarily, of their own free will, these people could also be assumed to have no difficulty in receiving the saying. That leaves the rest of us.

Can *you* receive this saying? If you were (or have been) put away by your mate for some reason other than fornication, do you believe you have the power to live the rest of your life without any desire for the opposite sex?

If your answer is ''No,'' then you are not a eunuch. If you are not a eunuch, does anyone else have the right to force you to live like one? No one but God. And there is no indication that your loving heavenly Father desires that for you. In fact, His Word states just the opposite, that it was He who created the male and female body and the sex drive. It was He who instituted marriage for the purpose of giving fulfillment to that natural God-given urge. It would seem, then, that it is not His intention for you or anyone else to be forced by custom or convention to spend a lifetime with that need unfulfilled.

Some Bible teachers seem to have the attitude: ''When you get a divorce, you ought to lose your sex drive.'' You know that doesn't happen. It's not right for any human being to try to force any other person into one of these three classifications of eunuchs.

Matthew 19:9 is not a law. A person doesn't establish a law and then turn right around and say, ''All men cannot receive this. Let those who can receive it, do so.'' If something is a law, it is to be received whether people like it or not.

The national 55-miles-per-hour speed limit is not a "saying" to be received "by them who can receive it." As the posters remind us: "55—it's not just a good idea, it's the LAW!" Someone has pointed out that when God handed down His laws to Moses, He didn't call them "The Ten Suggestions"!

The law applies to everyone or it applies to no one, that is the basic premise on which our whole system of democratic government is built. But this is not a law, it is a saying. Jesus knew that not everyone could live this strenuously. He did. Jesus lived the life of one of those "which have made themselves eunuchs for the Kingdom of heaven's sake." But He does not require or even ask that of everyone.

If a person is put away without cause, the first desire of his heart should be to try to reconcile his marriage. If that is not possible—and sometimes it just isn't—then he should consider making himself a eunuch for the Kingdom of heaven's sake. (The Apostle Paul talks about this in 1 Corinthians 7, which we will look at in the next chapter.) But it is not someone else's responsibility or privilege to require that decision of another person. That is a personal decision of the individual heart. If a person does not feel led to choose that way of life, then he does not fit into one of the three classifications of those who can receive this saying and should not be pressured to do so.

In that case, it is not a sin for that individual to remarry—in fact, he had better remarry! Unless he has the gift and call of making himself a eunuch for the Kingdom of God, he would do well to desire a second marriage partner. Otherwise his own natural gift of the sex drive will keep him in constant tension and vulnerable to Satan's wiles. Which is greater sin, to remarry, or to fall for sexual temptation?

A Third View

And he arose from thence, and cometh into the coasts of Judaea by the farther side of Jordan: and the people resort unto him again; and, as he was wont, he taught them again.

And the Pharisees came to him, and asked him, Is it lawful for a man to put away his wife? tempting him.

And he answered and said unto them, What did Moses command you?

And they said, Moses suffered to write a bill of divorcement, and to put her away.

And Jesus answered and said unto them, For the hardness of your heart he wrote you this precept.

But from the beginning of the creation God made them male and female.

For this cause shall a man leave his father and mother, and cleave to his wife;

And they twain shall be one flesh: so then they are no more twain, but one flesh.

What therefore God hath joined together, let not man put asunder.

And in the house his disciples asked him again of the same matter.

And he saith unto them, Whosoever shall put away his wife, and marry another, committeth adultery against her.

And if a woman shall put away her husband, and be married to another, she committeth adultery (against him).

Mark 10:1-12

Here in this passage we find several things new. For one thing, the Pharisees admit that Moses **suffered** (allowed the husband) **to write a bill of divorcement, and to put her** (the wife) **away**, rather than claiming that he "commanded" it. Secondly, we see that Jesus here speaks of the woman putting away her husband. Up to this point it has just been the man putting away his wife. Jesus believed in equality.

In Matthew 5, Matthew 19, and Mark 10 we have three slightly different statements attributed to Jesus. In Matthew 5:32 He is quoted as saying, "Whoever puts away his wife *causes her to commit adultery.*" In Matthew 19:9 He is said to say, "Whoever puts away his wife, *and marries another, commits adultery.*" In Mark 10:11 He is supposed to have said, "Whoever puts away his wife, and marries another, commits adultery *against her.*"

Now these three don't contradict one another. (There is a similar passage in Luke 16:18: **Whosoever putteth away his wife, and marrieth another, committeth adultery: and whosoever marrieth her that is put away from her husband committeth adultery**.) Though they do seem to be saying different things, all of the Gospel writers agree on one point: Whoever marries "her that is put away" commits adultery.

But let's look at this situation a bit closer. In Matthew 5, Jesus said that when a man puts away his wife, he *causes her* to commit adultery. We understand that to mean that the woman has been caused to commit adultery whether she remarries or not. We also understand that to refer to spiritual adultery. Now tie that statement in with what we have been saying about Matthew 19:9 being a "saying."

Matthew 19 does not contradict Matthew 5, but it doesn't add a great deal either. In Matthew 19 Jesus said that if a man puts away his wife and marries another, *he* commits adultery. Is it then that he *causes her* to commit adultery, or that *he himself* commits adultery? Which is it? In either case, this could still be referring to spiritual adultery relating to the divorce, instead of to remarriage.

Whether the man who puts away his wife causes her to commit apostasy—spiritual falling away—or whether he commits the apostasy, the result is the same. The putting away has caused a spiritual disturbance, a spiritual falling away.

But in Mark 10:11 it is phrased a little differently. Here the man who puts away his wife commits adultery *against her*. (There would be no difference if it were the woman who put away her husband. If she gets the divorce, she also commits adultery against him.)

Question: How could getting remarried be committing adultery against the person to whom one was formerly married? That new relationship does not have any physical impact at all on one's former mate. Therefore how in the world could getting remarried cause someone else to commit adultery?

The answer is simple. When a divorced person remarries, that marriage may not have any *physical* impact on his or her former mate, but it has a definite *spiritual* impact. The two original mates are no longer one in spirit. Now one of them has become one with another person, and that does matter. It does have consequences. When a person is put away because his or her mate wants to marry someone else, can you imagine the turmoil that is provoked in their spirit of unity? Can you see what that divorce and remarriage can generate spiritually—the strife, the hatred, the bitterness, the anguish in the life of the person put away?

Remarriage—Sin, or Salvation?

There are many Christians today who wear a mask to hide their true feelings. They come to church and smile at everyone. They look so lovely, so happy—on the outside. But inside they are hurt, or bitter, or destroyed, because someone has committed adultery against them. Somebody has generated problems for them in the realm of the spirit. Such people need to forgive. But they also need to be forgiven. That's where the Church comes in. Or does it?

There are people, Christian people, who will no longer have anything to do with God because someone has committed adultery against them. Someone has put them in such a state of spiritual turmoil that they have no interest in the things of God.

What has been the Church's attitude toward such hurting people?

"Well, it's too bad about your divorce. We're really sorry about it. But since you are divorced, we can't allow you to remarry. Remarriage is forbidden. According to the law, it's your duty now to live out the rest of your life single. It's regrettable that you can never again experience the fullness and joy we find in our marriage. We have a wonderful sexual relationship, and it's approved by God. But for you to get married again would be adultery. Sorry.''

Hypocrites!

I don't believe that Jesus ever meant for us to think of remarriage as adultery. I don't believe that Jesus ever meant for us to put the sexual connotations on His words that we have. Sure, if one person, husband or wife, becomes sexually involved with another person, that is grounds for divorce. That is very clear to me, as it should be to you. But I can't believe that Jesus ever meant to say that remarriage itself is immoral.

There is only one situation in which I would say that remarriage is wrong. If a person gets divorced in order to marry someone else, I would call that immoral. But even then the immorality would be in that person's heart, not in the remarriage. The sin was the motive, not the action.

I believe that Jesus' statements on this subject can be summarized this way: Divorce is wrong: it is not God's will or desire. The only justifiable grounds for divorce is sexual infidelity. If a person divorces his or her mate in order to marry someone else, that divorce and remarriage is adulterous. But remarriage—of itself—is not immoral.

5

Paul's View of
Marriage and Divorce

Know ye not that the unrighteous shall not inherit the Kingdom of God? Be not deceived: neither fornicators, nor idolaters, nor adulterers, nor effeminate, nor abusers of themselves with mankind,

Nor thieves, nor covetous, nor drunkards, nor revilers, nor extortioners, shall inherit the Kingdom of God.

1 Corinthians 6:9,10

So far in our discussion of marriage, divorce and adultery, we have considered the views of Moses, Jesus and the Gospel writers. Now let's see what the Apostle Paul, author of two-thirds of the New Testament, had to say on these vital issues. We will begin by looking at 1 Corinthians 6:9-20 and then continue our study by examining the entire chapter of 1 Corinthians 7. I realize this is a great deal of ground to cover, but I believe the importance of this subject to the Church of Jesus Christ today warrants such thorough investigation.

In this first passage we find a list of people who, according to Paul, will not inherit the Kingdom of God. He begins with the unrighteous in general, then goes on to enumerate the kinds of people who compose this ungodly group: fornicators, idolaters, homosexuals, thieves, drunkards, etc.

Are Christians included in this listing? Of course not. This same Paul teaches us that because of our faith in Christ Jesus, we have been made **the righteousness of God in him** (2 Cor. 5:21). If we are righteous, then we are not part of this group. But notice that list in verse 10.

Included among the unrighteous are adulterers. Now if in fact being put away or divorced causes a person to commit adultery, as the scriptures we have studied seem to say, then there must be some remedy for that condition. There has to be something which can be done about this sin of adultery. Either that or God does not hold this person responsible for being put away. Because this scripture says that no adulterer shall inherit the Kingdom of God.

If divorce makes a person an adulterer and there is nothing he can do to change that fact, then that person is doomed. He cannot inherit the Kingdom of God. But what if he had no choice in the matter? What if he did not want to be put away? Is that individual still destined to miss heaven because of someone else's decision? That does not sound like the God I serve. My God is not one to force anyone into a situation which causes him to commit adultery, and then condemns him to eternal banishment for doing so.

Fortunately there is something that person can do. Many people would suggest that in that case the only recourse the individual has is to talk his mate into reconciling their marriage; otherwise, they would say, both mates are adulterers forever.

A lot of people have tried to reconcile their marriage. Sometimes it works. But many times it doesn't.

What then? Is there no hope for the wronged party? Is his or her fate really sealed forever? Of course not. No one is ever condemned for the actions of another. Nor is any sinner, even an adulterer, beyond the scope of God's saving grace.

A divorced person's relationship with God has been hindered, even if he or she was put away unwillingly. But that situation can be overcome. There is something that can be done about it other than convincing the opposing mate to reconcile the marriage.

But what if the wronged mate has since remarried? Or what about the person who marries the wrongly divorced mate? To some people any marriage involving a divorced person is automatically adulterous. Quite frankly, I don't believe that is true. I don't believe that adultery occurs at the point of remarriage. I believe it occurs at the point of divorce. And by divorce I mean, of course, the tearing apart of the spirit of unity between a husband and wife. That division does not take place in court, as most people assume, but actually occurs in the hearts and minds of the two people involved, whether they ever physically separate or not.

If a person is put away, that person is not an adulterer—he is the victim of adultery. I firmly believe that the adultery spoken of by our Lord is not the sex act or immorality, but is in fact a spiritual matter. It is a falling away from God, a breaking fellowship with Him, a disturbance in relationship with the Father. If that divorced individual should remarry, the person who marries him or her will become involved in that spiritual disturbance.

I don't believe that Jesus was laying down a law when He gave us the statements which we have just studied. Rather He was putting us on notice. He was giving us warning of what would occur if we found ourselves involved in that particular situation called divorce. Jesus gave a lot of warnings of that nature. He didn't come to institute laws, as we have noted. He came to warn us of the consequences if we did not live our lives as God intended. I believe that purpose is consistent throughout His ministry, and I think we should look at this subject in that light.

Restored to Favor

And such were some of you: but ye are washed, but ye are sanctified, but ye are justified in the name of the Lord Jesus, and by the Spirit of our God.

1 Corinthians 6:11

So Paul has given us a long list of people who will not inherit the Kingdom of God. **And such were some of you,** he tells us. Is that true?

Among the people who will read this book, do you imagine there are some who were at one time or another unrighteous? Even you perhaps? And me? Of course. Every one of us was at some point in the past unrighteous. All of us. But it's quite possible, even probable, that among our readers some were involved in fornication, or (spiritual) idolatry, or adultery of some kind, maybe even some of these other vices as well. After all, the prerequisite for membership in the Church of Jesus Christ is to have been a sinner. No one else need apply. Isn't that right? And among a group as large as ours, there are bound to be representatives from all these classifications mentioned here.

Please note the tense of the verb in this verse. **And such *were* some of you: but** (now) **ye are washed, but** (now) **ye are sanctified, but** (now) **ye are justified in the name of the Lord Jesus, and by the Spirit of our God.**

Suppose a dope addict who has made Jesus the Lord of his life stood up in church and testified, "I used to be a dope addict, but not anymore. I have been washed, sanctified, justified in the name of the Lord Jesus and by the Spirit of God." What do you suppose would happen? Everyone would clap and say, "Oh, that's wonderful! He used to be a dope addict, but thank God, he's not anymore."

Now suppose that marvelous testimony was followed by this one: "I used to be an alcoholic, but not anymore. I made Jesus the Lord of my life, and now I'm washed, sanctified and justified." What would be the response? "Isn't that wonderful? He used to be an alcoholic, but he's not anymore."

But now suppose those joyous testimonies were followed by one like this: "I used to be married to John Doe, but we got a divorce, and now I am married to Bill Jones. I used to be guilty of adultery because I was put away by my first husband, but now I'm no longer guilty because I am washed, sanctified and justified in the name of the Lord Jesus and by the Spirit of God."

What response do you think that bit of truth might elicit from most good church members? Not quite the same as the first two, right? Hardly. Oh, we good Christians might accept this person back into the folds of the Church, but there might be a few stipulations, a few minor limitations placed on her activities, such as the fact that she would no longer be allowed to sing in the choir, teach a Sunday school class, lead in the women's missionary society, etc. And heaven forbid that she should dare to even think of preaching! Why? Is she any less washed, sanctified, justified than the first two?

And such WERE some of you, says Paul. That's past tense! If they were, then that means they are not anymore. All that past is forgiven and forgotten. Or is it?

Paul was writing here to former adulterers, homosexuals, drunkards, revilers, extortioners—all the fine upstanding folks down at the First Church of Corinth. If you know anything at all about the Corinthian church, you know that they were a bunch of immoral rascals. Oh, they spoke in tongues all right. (Too much, in fact, according to what we read in later chapters.) They interpreted tongues and gave forth many prophecies. They exercised the gifts of the Spirit exuberantly. But that doesn't mean their lives were morally clean.

The gifts of the Spirit are wonderful and are to be sought and exercised. But the gifts of the Spirit do not improve character. It takes the fruit of the Spirit to do that. If the gifts of the Spirit of God operated in anyone's life at any time in the past, or if they operate in any life in the future, it is not for that individual's own benefit, it is for the good and benefit of others. For personal benefit, it takes the fruit of that Spirit. And the fruit (the product) of the Spirit is quite different from the gift (the manifestation) of that Spirit.

So we see these Corinthian Christians carrying on in their same immoral way. Then why did Paul write

to them saying, "Some of you USED TO BE fornicators, idolaters, adulterers, but not anymore"? What
had happened to change all that? Did Paul hold some
kind of mass divorce service for all the "re-marrieds"
in that church?

Some people teach that the only way for a
divorced person to cancel the adultery caused by
divorce is to remarry his original mate. If he has remarried since the divorce, then the only recourse is to
divorce the second mate and be reconciled to the first.
Is that what had happened to these people? No, not
at all.

They were no longer fornicators, idolaters and
adulterers not because they had remarried their first
mates but because they had been washed, sanctified,
justified in the name of the Lord Jesus and by the Spirit
of God. Remarrying one's first mate doesn't sanctify
anyone. It is God who sanctifies, not ceremony. If you
are a child of God, you are *already* washed, sanctified,
justified.

"Oh," you may be thinking, "if you really knew
me, you wouldn't say that. I'm really not very
righteous."

No, you're not. Not of yourself, you're not. I don't
have to know you personally to know that. For no one
is righteous in and of himself. It is only in Christ that
anyone is made righteous. If you are in Him, then I
don't need to know you to be able to affirm that you
are washed, sanctified, justified.

If that righteousness is not a manifest reality in
your life, it is only because you have not received it.
It is there, it is available to you. All you have to do

is to receive it by faith. That's the whole Gospel message in a nutshell. That is the message of reconciliation of which Paul speaks in 2 Corinthians 5:19: "It was God (personally present) in Christ, reconciling and restoring the world to favor with Himself, not counting up and holding against [men] their trespasses [but cancelling them]; and committing to us the message of reconciliation—of the *restoration to favor*" (AMP).

Thank God, no one can keep you from being restored to favor with Him. Not your family, your friends, your enemies—not even your church or pastor! There is absolutely no one who can keep you from being washed, sanctified, justified, or who can keep you from enjoying all the freedom and joy of that blessed state of righteousness and fullness that is yours in Christ Jesus. If you are a born-again believer, even if you are divorced, even if you have been remarried, you are just as righteous in the eyes of God as anyone else. And don't let anyone convince you otherwise. Regardless of their title or position, don't allow anyone to ever make you feel guilty, inferior or unfit for service to your Lord just because you have failed. No true believer is more washed, sanctified, or justified than any other, although there are some who would like to think so.

Forgiveness or License?

Despite the fact that we have been restored by Christ to favor with God, that does not mean that God's grace and forgiveness gives us a license to divorce and remarry at will. Some people seem to have the philosophy that it is easier to get forgiveness than permission:

"Well, if what you say is true, that divorce is wrong but that God forgives, then I'll just do it anyway. Then I'll ask God to forgive me and everything will be all right."

No, I didn't say that "everything will be all right." I did say that divorce is wrong, and I did say that God forgives that wrong. I also indicated that we Christians should recognize that fact and change our attitude toward divorced and remarried people. But never have I advocated either divorce or remarriage. I never said they were approved of God. And I certainly never said that they didn't matter. On the contrary, I have repeatedly stressed the deep significance and far-reaching consequences of the separation of two spirits which have been made one by God Himself.

Some people are not concerned with whether or not God has said that divorce or remarriage is right or wrong. They just figure that forgiveness covers everything. If grace is so wonderful and so free and abundant, they say, that makes a lot of room for sin. Paul had to deal with this attitude and philosophy in his day:

> What shall we say then? Shall we continue in sin, that grace may abound? God forbid. How shall we, that are dead to sin, live any longer therein?
>
> **Romans 6:1,2**

As Christians we are not to take lightly the grace and forgiveness of God, or the precious blood of our Lord Jesus Christ which purchased that restoration to favor for us. In Hebrews 10:29 we read these sobering words:

> Of how sorer punishment, suppose ye, shall he be thought worthy, who hath trodden under foot the

Son of God, and hath counted the blood of the covenant, wherewith he *was sanctified,* an unholy thing, and hath done despite unto the Spirit of grace?

If you are contemplating divorce, be very careful that you not be found guilty of treading under foot the Son of God, of counting the blood of the Covenant, by which you were sanctified, an unholy thing, thus doing spite to God's Spirit of grace.

You may say, "But I'm being divorced by my mate, and there is nothing I can do about it."

How much time have you spent on your face before God about it? I am not trying to put you under condemnation. I am simply saying to you, don't take the world's attitude of, "So what?" Whatever the circumstances or cause of the problem in your marriage, do your best to set it right, especially if you have invested several years in it. Why throw all of that away and risk another one? Look for the good in your marriage, consider all the positive things in your union. Work out your problems before it is too late.

Granted, there are times when a marriage simply does not work out. I think it's time we were mature enough to realize and admit that. There are people among our church members who have been put away. There are some who have put a mate away. To all of them I would simply say, ask God to forgive you. Then accept that forgiveness and go on and make a new life for yourself. But if it has not come to that yet, don't let it. Don't ever contemplate divorce. As Paul says, **...make not provision for the flesh, to fulfill the lusts thereof** (Rom. 13:14), whether that lust is for a new mate, or simply for "freedom" from the one you now have.

All Things Are Not Expedient

All things are lawful unto me, but all things are not expedient: all things are lawful for me, but I will not be brought under the power of any.

Meats for the belly, and the belly for meats: but God shall destroy both it and them. Now the body is not for fornication, but for the Lord; and the Lord for the body.

And God hath both raised up the Lord, and will also raise up us by his own power.

Know ye not that your bodies are the members of Christ? shall I then take the members of Christ, and make them the members of an harlot? God forbid.

1 Corinthians 6:12-15

Your spirit has been made one with the Spirit of Christ. Spiritually you are one with Him. But look at this. Your relationship with Christ is not just spiritual. According to verse 15, your body is a member of His body. I have been emphasizing the fact that your relationship with your mate is spiritual, but now I want to show that your relationship is not *just* spiritual.

Having been involved with a certain large training center for a number of years, I have met a lot of single people who thought they could establish a marriage relationship solely on spiritual things, on a spiritual level alone: ''Oh, we have a wonderful relationship. We get together and talk about the Word. We pray, and we intercede, and we discuss the revelation knowledge God has given us. We have such a wonderful spiritual relationship that I know we are just perfect for each other.''

Well, does that prayer partner of yours have a job? Does he have any ambition? What are his plans for the future? What do you know about his background, his character, his habits? What does he like to eat? How often does he bathe? Does he have a family somewhere? What kind of terms is he on with them? Does he know anything besides his great revelation?

Is your prayer partner attractive? Does she take care of herself? How does she dress? Can she handle money? Does she know how to cook? How does she feel about children, about working outside the home? How does she get along with her parents, friends, roommate? Does she have any knowledge about anything besides the Sunday school quarterly?

Thank God for spiritual relationships. But marriage is not just spiritual—it is a blending of spirit, soul and body. So is our relationship with the Lord Jesus Christ: **Now if any man have not** *the Spirit of Christ,* **he is none of his...** (Rom. 8:9). **But we have** *the mind of Christ* (1 Cor. 2:16). **Now ye are** *the body of Christ...*(1 Cor. 12:27).

I have actually heard people say, ''Well, I've got a spiritual relationship with God, so He doesn't care what I do with this body.''

I beg to differ! Verse 15 says, **Know ye not that your bodies are the members of Christ? shall I then take the members of Christ, and make them the members of an harlot?** Ours is not just a spiritual relationship, either with God or with our mate.

I want you to see what is so wrong with immorality by a Christian. Now I am talking about sex. Sexual adultery by a Christian is wrong because it is the involvement of the body of Christ in an illicit union. If Jesus were with you in visible form, would you think of inviting Him to take part in sexual immorality? Of course not, perish the thought! Then why, as a born-again believer, would you think of doing such a thing yourself? Your body is a member of His body.

> **What? know ye not that he which is joined to an harlot is one body? for two, saith he, shall be one flesh.**
>
> **1 Corinthians 6:16**

You are one with the Lord Jesus. The Scriptures are very clear on that. The word translated "joined" here is the Greek verb *kollao* meaning "to *glue, i.e.* (pass. or reflex.) to *stick* (fig.):...keep company...."[1] That is different from the Greek word translated "joined" in Matthew 19:6 (**What therefore God hath joined together...**). That word is *suzeugnumi* which *Strong's* defines as "to *yoke together*...."[2] There is no comparison here: one statement is said in bold relief of the other. A man who is joined to a harlot becomes one *body* with her, whereas a man who is joined to his wife becomes one *flesh* with her. There is a distinction.

Despite what the world may say, there is a vast difference between being joined to a harlot and being one flesh in marriage. Just because two people live together and share a wonderful sex life does not make them one flesh in the eyes of God. Sex does not constitute marriage. That is the point that Paul is making in this scripture. He is showing the difference between being joined to a harlot and being made one flesh. To

---

[1]*Strong's*, p. 43 of Greek Dictionary.

[2]Ibid., p. 67.

be made one flesh means to be yoked together permanently.

God takes that physical union seriously—even the union between a man and a harlot, a woman who is not his wife and not about to become his wife. Not only is God seriously concerned about the union between a husband and wife, He is also seriously concerned about the physical union between two people who are not married and who have no intention of ever being so. Why? The answer is found in the next verse.

But he that is joined unto the Lord is one spirit.

1 Corinthians 6:17

Since a Christian's new spirit is one with the Spirit of God, everything he does with his physical body affects Him. Now think about that. Everything you do with your physical body affects God Himself. That ought to make you a little more mindful of where you go and what you do.

Flee Fornication

As Christians, if everything we do involves Christ then we understand Paul's admonition to us here to "flee fornication." In Ephesians 5:3 he writes of fornication, **...let it not be once named among you, as becometh saints.**

We ought to live such a "squeaky-clean" Christian life that no one would even think of ever accusing us of fornication or adultery. Why? Besides living in accordance with the will of our Father, preserving our reputation, and serving as a good example to others, is there any reason we should be on our guard against falling into sexual temptation? Yes, a very important reason (as if these first three weren't enough!). Paul says that every sin a person commits is **without the body,** but that whoever commits fornication **sinneth against his own body.**

Let me explain what he means. Lying, stealing, cheating, extortion, murder, drunkenness—all of those things are wrong. They break our fellowship with God. In addition, they place us in a position to hurt others even more than ourselves. All this list of things, and manymore that we could name, have as much or more of an impact on the people we do them to as they do on us. But fornication is a sin against our own body. And that does not mean just against our physical body.

We are inclined to think that the body of Christ is our body. We need to realize that our body is also the body of Christ. You and I—individually—are the body of Christ. It's not as though the body of Christ is something that is already in existence which Jesus is going to share with us. No, we *are* the body of Christ. Without us, He has no body. That is a different way of looking at this concept. I believe it is the right way. Once you see yourself that way, then you understand that when you are guilty of committing fornication, it is a sin against your own body—not the body you can pinch—but against your Christian body.

Glorify God in Your Body

What? know ye not that your body is the temple of the Holy Ghost which is in you, which ye have of God, and ye are not your own?

> **For ye are bought with a price: therefore glorify God in your body, and in your spirit, which are God's.**
>
> 1 Corinthians 6:19-20

There is a philosophy making the rounds today which holds that sexual relationship between two "consenting adults" is acceptable, even deeply "meaningful"—provided, of course, that the two parties "really care about each other." What do you suppose the reaction of the Apostle Paul would be to that assertion? "WHAT? DON'T YOU KNOW THAT YOU ARE THE TEMPLE OF THE HOLY GHOST? Have you forgotten that you are not your own? You've been bought with a price!"

And what a price was paid for us! When we sin against our own body, we sin against the temple of the Holy Ghost. Do you have any idea of the penalty in Old Testament days for profaning the temple of the Most High God? Yet many believers today act as though that sacred temple means nothing to them. It is a very inappropriate thing for the temple of the Holy Ghost to be used as a house of prostitution. Wouldn't you agree?

You and I have no right to treat our body in such a way as to bring shame and dishonor upon our Lord. Why? Because God bought that body. It is now His. If it belongs to God, we ought to be very careful how we use the property of the Holy One of Israel!

Despite what so many people seem to think, our body is not ours to do with as we please. It belongs to God who paid a terrible price to redeem it for us. Why? What is our body for? In verse 20, Paul says it is to be used to "glorify God." Are you glorifying God in your body?

Some time ago I suddenly realized I was not glorifying God in my body. Not because I was engaging in sexual immorality, but because I was 30 pounds overweight. I found that I was having a tough time physically doing all the things God was telling me to do. With the heavy schedule I keep, traveling and ministering constantly, I discovered that when I began to minister under a heavy, tangible anointing, I could hardly last 10 minutes. That extra weight was sapping me of the energy and vitality I need to minister effectively for the Lord. The Spirit of God spoke to me quite clearly and revealed to me that I needed to lose that 30 pounds of excess weight which was hindering me in my service to Him.

Did I do it?

I most certainly did. But I didn't do it by going on some "lose-weight-fast" fad diet or by making reservations at some expensive "fat farm." I didn't take dangerous diet pills or have my mouth wired shut. I simply decided that my excess weight was not glorifying to God, and so I resolved that with His help I was going to change that situation. I sat down and worked out a sensible weight-loss program which I followed conscientiously over a period of time. I cut out all the excesses, replacing all the rich, calorie-loaded junk I used to eat with wholesome, nutritious foods. I ate less and less often. In short, I changed my eating habits. As a result, I gradually lost those extra pounds and in the process gained not only a new physique but new energy and a new sense of self-respect and self-esteem.

Self-respect. *Self*-esteem. That's what God wants for us. That's why He wants us to glorify Him in our body. He knows that we need those intangible things just as much as, if not more than, we do the new body we develop.

That's what Paul is telling us here. He is exhorting us as Christians, whether ministers or lay people, to take authority over our body, to bring it into submission, to control it rather than allowing it to control us. Whatever we do—whether eating, drinking, sleeping, exercising, relaxing, working, worshipping or lovemaking—in all of our mental, physical and spiritual activities, we ought to glorify our Lord whose we are and whom we serve.

6

Harmony of the Word

In this last chapter we are going to continue studying the viewpoint of the Apostle Paul in regard to marriage and divorce, concentrating particularly on the seventh chapter of 1 Corinthians. In so doing I will attempt not only to summarize Paul's statements, but also to show how his New Testament teaching harmonizes perfectly with what we have previously learned from Jesus, the Gospel writers, and the Mosaic Law. There is no real conflict here in these teachings, rather a progressive revelation of God's Word to us on a subject which He knew would become in our day a vital issue of concern to all—**especially unto them who are of the household of faith** (Gal. 6:10).

Is Sex a Sin?

Now concerning the things whereof ye wrote unto me: It is good for a man not to touch a woman.

Nevertheless, to avoid fornication, let every man have his own wife, and let every woman have her own husband.

1 Corinthians 7:1

Apparently this epistle was written by Paul in response to a letter he had received from the church in Corinth in which they had posed certain questions relating to Christian life. Seemingly one of the questions was this: Is sex a sin?

Now that may seem like a rather silly question. But if it is so ridiculous then why are so many people still asking it?

Is sex a sin? Let's look at Paul's answer: **It is good for a man not to touch a woman.** Notice that he does not say that it is good for a husband not to touch his wife. This was not a blanket condemnation of sex. On the contrary, as we will see, Paul believed in and heartedly endorsed the sexual relationship in marriage. What he was warning against is sexual involvement outside of marriage. In that case, Paul would affirm, yes, sex is wrong. Always was, always will be. Nothing will ever change that. No matter how sophisticated or "enlightened" we may become in our modern society, extra-marital sex will never be acceptable behavior in the eyes of God.

There are many people today who call themselves Christians yet who no longer accept that premise. They seem to feel that modern man has progressed beyond (what is to them) such a "narrow-minded" view. Such people are wrong. On this one issue Paul spoke very clearly God's viewpoint: **...Avoid fornication.** That should be straightforward enough for even the most liberal-minded of saints to grasp.

Defraud Not One Another

But in this "liberated" age in which sex is viewed so casually and in which temptation is so prevalent, how are we to avoid fornication? The answer is found in verse 2: **...to avoid fornication, let every man have his own wife, and let every woman have her own husband.** In other words, God's answer to the sex question is simple: get married!

We must remember that marriage was God's idea. One of the purposes of marriage is to provide a lawful and legitimate release and fulfillment of the sex urge which is found in every normal, healthy human being. It's just that simple.

We have read where Jesus said as much in His response to this same question put to Him: **But from the beginning of the creation God made them male and female.** *For this cause* **shall a man leave his father and mother, and cleave unto his wife; and they twain shall be one flesh** (Mark 10:6-8). For what cause? Because they *are* male and female. God knew what making them male and female would produce. That's why He also created and instituted marriage, to provide a means of gratifying the natural desires which would come about as a result of their being male and female! That's what marriage is for. At least, that is one of its purposes. As we see in verse 3:

> **Let the husband render unto the wife due benevolence: and likewise also the wife unto the husband.**

Plainly stated, this means that the husband and wife should meet each other's need. The husband should fulfill his wife's sexual needs, and the wife should satisfy her husband's sexual hunger. That is why God created them male and female, to complement (complete, fulfill) each other in every way. Sex is not just something a husband and wife do *with* each other—it is also something they do *for* each other.

111

The wife hath not power of her own body, but the husband: and likewise also the husband hath not power of his own body, but the wife.

Defraud ye not one the other, except it be with consent for a time, that ye may give yourselves to fasting and prayer; and come together again, that Satan tempt you not for your incontinency.

1 Corinthians 7:4,5

What God is saying here through the Apostle Paul is that one of the major reasons for marriage is so that the wife can meet the sexual needs of the husband, and the husband can meet the sexual needs of the wife. He emphasizes that the need fulfillment aspect of marriage is so important, so significant, that to refuse to meet that need is to defraud one's partner. The only exception to this rule is when **both** parties agree to abstain for a time in order to devote themselves totally to fasting and prayer.

But then Paul gives us this warning: "Come together again, so Satan cannot tempt you." How many marriages have been broken up because one of the partners became so "heavenly minded" he or she was no earthly good! Whenever one mate refuses to meet the needs of the other, that is an open invitation to Satan to move in and tempt that individual to sin. Then the one who does get involved in immorality gets all the blame. God says that unless the two partners *mutually* agree differently, sex is to be a vital part of that marriage. No marriage partner ever has the right to withhold sex from his or her mate. That is expressly forbidden.

One time a certain woman came to talk with a pastor friend of mine about her marriage. In the course of the conversation the lady revealed that she was teaching her husband "self-discipline."

"What do you mean?" asked my friend.

"Well," the lady explained, "I've just decided that Joe needs to learn self-discipline, so I'm withholding sex from him until he does."

"Oh, and how long have you been doing this?"

"About a year now, I guess."

"Well, Ma'am, I hate to disappoint you," my friend told the lady. "But you're not teaching your husband self-discipline, you're teaching him a new trick."

"What new trick?"

"Not to come home at night!"

Despite that lady's "good intentions," she was not teaching her husband anything. What she was actually doing was defrauding him.

To Marry or Not to Marry

For I would that all men were even as I myself. But every man hath his proper gift of God, one after this manner, and another after that.

1 Corinthians 7:7

Now doesn't that strike a note of familiarity? In Matthew 19:10-12, Jesus spoke of His teaching on the subject of remaining single: **All men cannot receive this saying, save they to whom it is given.... He that is able to receive it, let him receive it** (vv. 11,12).

Here Paul says: "I would like for everyone to be like me (unmarried), but every man has his own gift of God." They are both saying exactly the same thing:

113

"If you don't desire to get married, if you have no need for marriage, stay single. If you can't remain single, get married. Celibacy is not every person's gift."

Notice that Paul doesn't make any reference to why some people are single, why some remain unmarried, but he does begin to clarify it a little in verse 8:

> **I say therefore to the unmarried and widows, It is good for them if they abide even as I.**

Please don't read anything extra into this statement. We know that Paul is speaking to those who are single, to the unmarried and widows. That much is clear. He is saying to them, "If you have this gift of God and are comfortable with it, if it's fine with you to stay single, then remain that way."

At this point in time Paul is obviously not married because he says it is good for the single to remain "even as I." Was he ever married? Or was he always single? Is it possible that Paul had been married and his wife had died? Or is it even possible that the great apostle of the faith was divorced? We don't know. All we know is that he is not married at the time of this writing.

Let's compare 1 Corinthians 6:12 with 1 Corinthians 7:8. In that former verse Paul wrote, **All things are lawful unto me, but all things are not expedient: all things are lawful for me, but I will not be brought under the power of any.** In the latter verse he writes, "It is good for single people to remain unmarried, as I have done." In other words, Paul was saying, "I could get married if I wanted to. I haven't remained single because some law says I can't get married. My marital status is *my* business—and my *decision*. It's just more expedient for me to remain single than to marry."

Paul made a decision not to be brought under the power of anything. On the basis of that decision he had made another one: that he would remain unmarried. Those decisions were made as acts of Paul's own free will, not as required observances of law. Paul is not speaking of Mosaic Law here. There is nothing in this chapter that even vaguely relates to Law. Jesus fulfilled that Law, and Paul knew it. The only law now left in effect is the Law of Love. That Law of love was operating so completely in Paul's life that he was in total control. He was not going to be brought under the power of anything else. There is no legalism involved here. Whatever Paul did, he did out of love—not out of obligation or duty. It seems obvious that he would grant that same right and freedom he enjoyed to any other born-again believer.

> **But if they cannot contain, let them marry: for it is better to marry than to burn.**
>
> **1 Corinthians 7:9**

You know, there are a lot of people who think that in this seventh chapter of 1 Corinthians Paul was making continuous reference to the difficulty of the times. That's supposedly why he was encouraging these people not to get married. I don't believe that. The devil is the same today as he was 2,000 years ago. And he was the same devil 2,000 years before that. Ever since the fall of man, Satan has been the same and has been doing the same devilish things. I don't think that Paul was so moved by the particular time in which he lived that this formed the basis for the statements he makes here.

Some people try to explain away this entire chapter by saying that Paul knew how hard it was going to be for those people to keep the faith with all of the persecution they were going to have to face, so he was advising them that it would be better for them to remain single because they could handle hard times better that way.

Well, if that's what he was talking about, I beg to differ with Paul. I know from my own experience, and I am sure you will agree, that hard times are the very time we need the strength and support and comfort of loved ones, especially our mate. Being married does not make one any less capable of facing hardship. If anything, it makes him more able to do so. There is strength in numbers, power in unity.

But I am persuaded that that was not what Paul was saying. Circumstances were never Paul's primary concern. If there was ever a man who had opportunity to be concerned about circumstances, it was Paul. When we consider his persecutions, imprisonments, shipwrecks, beatings, stonings, hardships of every kind, we can see right away that if there was ever a person who had a right to consider such things, it was the Apostle Paul.

But he could not have cared less about circumstances. He shook them off like he shook off the snake from his hand on the island of Melita. (Acts 28:3-5.) To Paul all these things were mere "light affliction" (2 Cor. 4:17), and not worthy of note. He says it was his policy to forget those things which were behind and to press on toward the mark of the high calling in Christ Jesus. (Phil. 3:13.)

Well, if Paul wasn't concerned about circumstances, what was he concerned about? About getting the Gospel out! His interest was in seeing the Good News of Jesus Christ spread throughout the then-known world.

Then why does he make these statements about remaining single? What has that to do with spreading the Gospel?

Quite simple. It is easier for a single person to "go into all the world" than it is for a married person. The single person does not have the entanglements and obligations that a married person has. Especially a married person with a family either to provide for or to take care of in the home.

Paul's concern wasn't with survival, it was with conquest! He simply wanted as many Christians as possible to be free to go wherever and whenever the Lord might lead.

But some people can't do that. They have to remain rooted and tied where they are. And others can't do that unless they do have a mate. Some men need the comfort and support of a good wife. Just as some women need the strength and protection of a good husband. That's not being "sexist," it's being honest.

Some men, like some women, need a partner. They need to function as a team. There are many

Christians today who are completely ineffective, totally useless to the Kingdom of God simply because they need to get married. Now I didn't say that a person couldn't do anything in the Kingdom of God unless he or she was married. The two people who have done the most in that Kingdom were single: Jesus and Paul. But I said that there are some people who will never be able to do anything for God unless they *get* married. Because their mind is too caught up with other things. They are hindered, bothered by other considerations. Usefulness to the kingdom was Paul's concern. It should be ours also.

To Remarry or Not to Remarry

But if they cannot contain, let them marry: for it is better to marry than to burn.

There are some people who would take issue with me when I say that a divorced person can do more for the Kingdom of God by getting remarried than by remaining single. My basis for that statement is 1 Corinthians 7:9. I know this was originally directed at "the unmarried and widows," but I am convinced that Paul's admonition to "the unmarried" applies just as much to the divorced as it does to those who have never been married.

And unto the married I command, yet not I, but the Lord, Let not the wife depart from her husband:

But and if she depart, let her remain unmarried, or be reconciled to her husband: and let not the husband put away his wife.

1 Corinthians 7:10,11

118

These statements agree exactly with what Jesus said. Simply stated: If you're married, stay married; don't get a divorce. But if you do get a divorce, remain unmarried or be reconciled to your mate.

But there is something which needs to be clarified here. I have said it before, but it bears repeating. Divorce does not change the needs and desires that marriage was created to meet. God did not create and institute marriage for no reason. It was not just something He dreamed up on the spur of the moment. Marriage has a purpose. Many purposes, in fact.

We have already seen that one of these purposes is to provide a means of fulfillment of the sex drive in the human male and female. That purpose does not change when divorce occurs. Neither do the needs of men and women. If every other legitimate means of meeting those needs is wrong, is sinful, then what kind of God would refuse remarriage to the divorced person, thereby denying him or her forever the lifelong privilege of having their most basic needs met?

But I would like to make a stronger statement than that. What kind of God would refuse the divorced person the lifelong privilege of meeting someone else's needs? It is a far greater, more significant thing to meet someone else's needs than it is to have one's own needs met. Our Lord Jesus taught that it is better to give than to receive. Ours is not the kind of God who would put a person in a position where he could not have his needs met. After everything God has said in His Word about giving, He certainly wouldn't place an individual in a position in which he could never again the rest of his whole life have the opportunity to meet someone else's needs.

In verses 10 and 11 Paul exhorts believers not to divorce, but if that does happen, to be reconciled to their mate if at all possible. That is first priority. In fact, if you are divorced, the greatest reason to remain unmarried is to hold on to the possibility of being reconciled with your former mate.

How Long to Wait

But how long should a person wait for that reconciliation? The rest of his or her life?

We have already discussed scriptures that make it clear that if that mate remarries, there is no point in waiting any longer. Even if the second mate should die or be divorced, it would be an abomination to God for the first two partners to remarry.

Then what should you do if you and your mate have already remarried after one of you was married to someone else? Should you then get divorced? Heaven forbid! Two divorces do not make a right. In that case, simply ask God's forgiveness for your mistakes and then go on and make a new life for yourselves in peace and harmony with each other and in accordance with God's will for your lives together. Love and serve God just as though you had never been apart. Others who know of the situation may not understand or approve, but that doesn't really matter. You and God understand, and that is enough.

But suppose two people are divorced and are not remarried. How long should the Christian wait for his or her mate to reconcile the marriage?

There have been divorced people who have told me, "I have been divorced now for 5 years. I'm still believing God that my marriage will be reconciled. I still have hope—but how much longer should I wait?"

Others have said, "I've lost all hope of my mate ever reconciling our marriage. There is no indication that there is any love for me there at all. How long should I wait?"

While still others have grimly stated, "I am divorced from my mate, but the Bible says to wait. Therefore I am waiting because I have to. I just wish I knew how long I have to wait before I can finally be set free from this thing."

If you are divorced and are considering that question, I will tell you exactly how long to wait. *As long as you love your mate.* If you are waiting because of some legalistic thing, your waiting is doing no good. The Bible says that faith works by love. (Gal. 5:6.) Faith does not work by law, but by love. If you love that person and are believing for a reconciliation, the thing that makes your faith work is your love for him or her. Once that love is gone, faith is in vain and waiting is useless.

There are so many people today who only wait. Five years. Seven years. Ten years. Usually they wait because to them this statement by Paul is a law, one they dare not disobey. Perhaps they have never believed their marriage will be restored. Even if they do want it to be, hope it will be, believe it will be, their believing is not working because they don't love their mate any longer. They don't wait hopefully, confidently, expectantly, out of love—but doggedly, stubbornly, negatively, out of a sense of duty or obligation. Such people, sad to say, wait in vain.

I have asked divorced people, "Do you love the person you are divorced from?"

Many times the response will be, "Well, I don't really know after the way I've been treated. I used to, but I'm not sure I do now. But I'm not going to get remarried because the Bible says to remain unmarried. So I've just got to wait and hope my mate and I can get back together. Even though I'm not sure I really want that, or really believe it will ever happen—which I don't."

There's no faith in that. And there's no love in that. If you are in that situation and are approaching it from such a legalistic standpoint, there is nothing there to make your faith work. If you really love your divorced mate, if you really want your marriage reconciled, then take a stand of faith on that love and desire. Ask God to restore your marriage. Then do your part to see that it really happens by putting dynamic, love-grounded faith to work on your behalf. Unless your faith is alive and active and working in love, unless it is greater and stronger than your mate's lack of faith and love, then all the waiting in the world won't do you or your mate a bit of good.

It's not how long you wait. It's what you *do* while you are waiting that counts.

So in conclusion, we might summarize this point by saying: If you have to ask, "How long do I wait?" you may as well quit waiting now. Unless your love for your mate is so strong that you are *resolved* to see that thing through until your marriage is restored no matter how long that takes, then your waiting is in vain.

Marriage With Unbelievers

But to the rest speak I, not the Lord: If any brother hath a wife that believeth not, and she be pleased to dwell with him, let him not put her away.

And the woman which hath an husband that believeth not, and if he be pleased to dwell with her, let her not leave him.

For the unbelieving husband is sanctified by the wife, and the unbelieving wife is sanctified by the husband: else were your children unclean; but now are they holy.

But if the unbelieving depart, let him depart. A brother or a sister is not under bondage in such cases: but God hath called us to peace.

1 Corinthians 7:12-15

But to the rest speak I.... Here Paul is not quoting from Jesus' teachings. He makes it clear that this is a revelation he has received directly from God. This is Paul's commentary which the Lord gave him personally on the subject of marriage, divorce, and remarriage. This is Paul, by the inspiration of the Holy Spirit, telling us believers on this side of Calvary how to live out what Jesus taught before Calvary.

One of the greatest mistakes the Church has made in comparing what Jesus said with what Paul said is in neglecting to recognize that Jesus spoke to the Jews before the cross while Paul spoke to the Gentiles after the cross. That difference is significant.

The Jews were a legalistic people. Their whole life was the Law. In speaking to them Jesus had to talk in legal terms like divorce, put away, adultery, and fornication. He could not use the faith terms like brother, believer, unbelieving, and sanctified which the Apostle Paul used because His listeners would not have understood what He was talking about.

The Jews who heard Jesus were not born again. Jesus knew that. But He also knew that they understood perfectly well the double meaning of the word adultery. Whether we understand that or not, the Jews did. They knew that the Hebrew and Greek words which we translate adultery indicated not only immorality but apostasy. Jesus knew they understood that the word fornication meant not only sexual intercourse, but idolatry. After all, for the last several hundred years, their own prophets and judges had been declaring to these people that they had gone "whoring" after other gods and had been committing "fornication"—(adultery, idolatry)—with the gods of other nations. Jesus was aware that the Jews of His day understood very well the spiritual implications and definitions of terms like adultery and fornication. That's why He spoke of marriage and divorce as He did. Like any good public speaker, He used language suited to the social, cultural and educational level of His listeners.

So did Paul. But Paul's audience was different from that of Jesus. They were much more able to relate to spiritual matters on a spiritual level than were the pre-crucifixion Jews. So what Paul actually does here in these verses is to translate Jesus' statements from legal terminology to faith terminology. Paul is writing to us Christian believers, so he uses language suited to our level of comprehension. But the basic teaching is the same. It is just expressed in different terms and symbols because it is aimed at a different audience in a different time and situation.

In fact, the whole message of the Bible from Genesis and Deuteronomy down through the Gospels and on through Paul's writings is fundamentally the same. God does not say one thing in one part of His Word and then say something different in another part. God's Word (His message to us) is not contradictory. But it is *progressive*. As we move through His Word from beginning to end, God opens to us a fuller revelation of His truth. That truth is the same, but our understanding of it deepens as we progress from line to line, precept to precept.

So with that concept in mind, let's examine what Paul had to say about marriage with an unbeliever. We remember that in 2 Corinthians 6:14 Paul warns believers: **Be ye not unequally yoked together with unbelievers: for what fellowship hath righteousness with unrighteousness? and what communion hath light with darkness?** Yet though he spoke out against marriage between believers and unbelievers, note that Paul did not condemn any believer who was thus "unequally yoked"—(which should give us some idea of what his viewpoint would be today on this whole issue of divorced people and remarriage)—nor did he advocate dissolving that union.

But to the rest speak I, not the Lord: If any brother hath a wife that believeth not, and she be pleased to dwell with him, let him not put her away. Does that call to your mind anything we have studied thus far? Do you remember our basic beginning lesson text from Deuteronomy 24:1? **When a man hath taken a wife,**

and married her, and it come to pass that she *find no favour in his eyes....* Compare that with this statement by Paul written hundreds of years later, after the crucifixion and resurrection of Christ: **If any brother hath a wife that believeth not, and** *she be pleased to dwell with him....*

Do you see the same type of thought expressed here, only reversed? In Deuteronomy a man could divorce his wife if she did not "find favour" in his eyes, in other words, if she wasn't "pleasing" to him. Here, a man who has a wife is cautioned not to put her away (even if she is not a believer), if she is "pleased" to dwell with *him*.

That is seemingly a total reversal of the Jewish Law. Or is it? Isn't it instead evidence of the fulfillment of the Jewish Law, which Jesus came to perform? Now there is *equality* before the Law. Now the woman has the same rights—and responsibilities—as the man, as borne out by verse 13: **And the woman which hath an husband that believeth not, and if he be pleased to dwell with her, let her not leave him.**

So here we see that a Christian, whether male or female, is not to divorce. If his or her mate is a believer, the two are one in flesh, one in spirit, one in Christ. If the mate is not a believer, then the Christian is not free to divorce as long as the unbelieving mate desires to remain married. Either way, the Christian marriage partner is not free to divorce, except in the case of marital infidelity, or unless the unbelieving mate puts him or her away.

So, even if one of the mates is not a believer, God still recognizes and blesses that union. Why? Why is the Christian husband or wife not to divorce an unbelieving mate who desires to remain in union? The answer is found in verse 14: **For the unbelieving husband is sanctified by the wife, and the unbelieving wife is sanctified by the husband: else were your children unclean; but now are they holy.**

I was talking to a man one day who was not a believer. This man said to me: ''You know, my wife and I used to go out partying every weekend. We'd go from bar to bar and get drunk—we just had a ball. Then my wife got religion and joined that church you belong to. Now she won't go out drinking with me anymore.''

''Oh, really?'' I answered.

''Yep,'' he said. ''So for a while I went by myself, but I soon got tired of that. Without my wife along, it was just no fun. So I don't go anymore. I just stay home on the weekends now, maybe drink a few beers, watch a little television.''

''Now don't you dare tell her this,'' he cautioned earnestly, leaning over close to confide in me, ''but here lately it's got to where my beer don't even taste good no more!''

''Oh, don't worry,'' I assured him. ''I won't say a word to her about it.'' I told the truth. I didn't have to say anything. That man's wife had already shared the situation with me.

''When I got saved,'' she told me, ''my husband didn't want me to go to church at all. Every time I went, he would get mad. But as time went on, he must have accepted the fact that I was going to go, because he quit putting up such a racket about it.''

"Then one day the strangest thing happened," she said. "My husband came home late from work one Wednesday night, and I wasn't dressed for prayer meeting like I usually am by that time. When he asked me about it, I told him I wasn't going that night, I was going to stay home with him. 'Oh, no, you're not!' he said. 'You're going to prayer meeting. Since you started going to that church down there, you're a better wife. Now you get yourself in there and get dressed. I don't want you to be late!' "

What was happening? Because of the faithfulness of the wife, that unbelieving husband was gradually being separated from the world, set apart unto God, and he didn't even know it. Isn't that wonderful? That's the purpose of dwelling with the unbelieving mate. If he or she is pleased to dwell with the believer, then the two should remain together, says Paul. I agree.

...else were your children unclean; but now are they holy. When a believer is married to an unbeliever, usually the believer's greatest concern is for the children of that union. While Paul does not, as many people mistakenly believe, offer here a *guarantee* that those children will be saved, he does assure Christians of the powerful influence they have on their children. It is more powerful than the influence of the unbeliever. It can result in their salvation. This same idea is carried over into verse 16 in regard to the salvation of the mate:

> **For what knowest thou, O wife, whether thou shalt save thy husband? or how knowest thou, O man, whether thou shalt save thy wife?**

Many Christians have been taught that they are to remain married to their unbelieving mate because unless they do so that mate cannot be saved. But, of course, that is not so. Paul never meant to imply that either the salvation of the children or of the mate was totally contingent upon that marriage union. What he does counsel is, if the unbelieving mate is content with the marriage, the Christian should not be the cause of its being dissolved. If that mate chooses to depart, however, the Christian should not resist his or her leaving.

The Choice Is Yours

But as God hath distributed to every man, as the Lord hath called every one, let him walk. And so ordain I in all churches.

1 Corinthians 7:17

Jesus said something similar to this, didn't He? He said that the person who could receive His saying on marriage was the one who should receive it. Here Paul says the same thing about his statements. After all, notice that it is the Lord who calls people to one kind of life or the other, not men. What you choose to do about your marital status is between you and God, not between you and other people, as well-intentioned as they may be. The choice is *yours*.

Be True to Your Calling

Is any man called being circumcised? let him not become uncircumcised.

Is any called in uncircumcision? Let him not be circumcised. Circumcision is nothing, and uncircum-

**cision is nothing, but the keeping of the command-
ments of God.**

1 Corinthians 7:18,19

There are many Christians who think that unless
they can get everybody else to believe and behave just
like them, those other people are not really Christian.
But neither doctrine nor behavior is the truly important thing. Paul says that what really matters is **the
keeping of the commandments of God.**

What commandments? The two greatest
commandments of our Lord were these: **...Thou shalt
love the Lord thy God with all thy heart, and with
all thy soul, and with all thy mind,** and, **Thou shalt
love thy neighbor as thyself** (Matt. 22:37,39). Nothing
is more important to us as Christians than this Law
of Love: That we love one another as Jesus loved us.
(John 13:34.) If we love one another, we will not judge,
criticize or condemn one another. Rather, we will allow
each person to fulfill the calling of God upon his or
her own individual life.

**Let every man abide in the same calling wherein he
was called.**

1 Corinthians 7:20

It is God who calls, not us. We need to remember
that our job is not to *live* other people's lives for them,
but to *love* other people as they are.

As for ourselves, Paul counsels us to remain true
to our own individual calling. In other words, no one
should feel he has to marry, divorce or remarry against
his own better judgment. Let God determine that for
you, not custom, tradition, church doctrine or public
opinion.

130

> **Art thou called being a servant? care not for it:**
> **but if thou mayest be made free, use it rather.**

> *1 Corinthians 7:21*

Whatever your calling might be, use it. For what? To spread the Gospel. If you can do that more effectively by remaining single, remain single. If you can do it better by being married, then get married.

> **For he that is called in the Lord, being a servant,**
> **is the Lord's freeman: likewise also he that is called,**
> **being free, is Christ's servant. Ye are bought with a**
> **price; be not ye the servants of men.**

> **Brethren, let every man wherein he is called**
> **abide in God.**

> *1 Corinthians 7:22-24*

As a Christian, you belong to God, so don't get caught up in what is going to please man. You are to please the One to whom you belong. Your decisions in life may not be understood or approved of by others, especially other Christians. Don't worry about it. Just love, accept and forgive them. But be true to what you know to be God's will and plan for your life.

Abide with God. Live your life in such a way that your fellowship with God will not be broken regardless of what men may think.

Good to be Faithful

> **Now concerning virgins I have no commandment**
> **of the Lord: yet I give my judgment, as one that hath**
> **obtained mercy of the Lord to be faithful.**

> **I suppose therefore that this is good for the**
> **present distress, I say, that it is good for a man so to**
> **be.**

> **Art thou bound unto a wife? seek not to be loosed. Art thou loosed from a wife? seek not a wife.**
>
> **But and if thou marry, thou hast not sinned; and if a virgin marry, she hath not sinned. Nevertheless such shall have trouble in the flesh: but I spare you.**
>
> **1 Corinthians 7:25-28**

In these verses Paul said he had no specific commandment of the Lord in regard to virgins, but he gave us his own judgment, which can be interpreted simply "to be faithful." By now, of course, that should be obvious, even to the carnal Christians in Corinth. Paul was saying to them that there was no law that an unmarried person had to remain single, or to marry—only to refrain from fornication or sexual immorality.

But note carefully that Paul did say in verse 28, **...if a virgin marry, she hath not sinned.**

What Paul is trying to do here is to establish balance. Corinth was a wretched place, a very sensuous city. All the Corinthians seemed to think about and indulge in was sex—fornication, homosexuality, lesbianism, incest, all possible forms of uncleanness.

They were marrying and giving in marriage, divorcing and being divorced, separating and remarrying. All this went on continually. Even in the Church. The Corinthian believers would gather together in church to prophesy, speak in tongues and interpret, to worship God exuberantly. But their Christianity didn't seem to extend far past the walls of the church. Certainly, it had not yet lessened their worldliness. Paul was writing to these people in an effort to help them understand that being free from the Jewish Law did not give them a license to live in debauchery.

Sad to say, many of our modern-day churches need this same message. We live in a world that needs to hear the Gospel of Christ. And we Christians are the ones with the answer. By what are we doing? We're acting just as bad as, if not worse than, the ones who are destined for destruction. We have been put on this earth to be a light to the world, to show them the Lord Jesus. What we've actually shown them is that we are no different from them.

There must be a balance. We *are* free from law, Jewish Law, man's law, but we are not free from the Law of Love, God's Law. If we love the world, as God so loved the world, we dare not allow ourselves to present a bad example to it, a false representation of what a Christian really is.

As Paul says, ''All things are lawful to us, but not all things are expedient.'' Expedient to what? To the spreading of the glorious Gospel of Jesus Christ which sets men free from the Law of sin and death. For our own sakes, and for the sake of the Gospel, let's not fall into sin. Let's be faithful.

Art thou bound unto a wife? seek not to be loosed. Art thou loosed from a wife? seek not a wife. But and if thou marry, thou hast not sinned. Are you married? If so, don't seek a divorce. Are you divorced? Then don't go looking for someone else to marry. That seems clear enough, doesn't it? But look at the next sentence. **But if thou marry, *thou hast not sinned....*** That ought to settle once and for all the question of whether remarriage is forbidden to a Christian. It is not.

Someone might say, ''But doesn't that refer to virgins, people who have never been married before?''

No. Paul's very next words were, **...and if a virgin marry, she hath not sinned.** If he had been referring to virgins in the first statement, there would have been no need for the second.

"Well then, if Paul was talking about remarriage, why didn't he use the word remarry?"

Because it wasn't necessary, for one thing. Let's think together for a minute. Is divorce a sin? If so, does God forgive that sin? When God forgives sin, does He also forget it? Then if a divorced person has been forgiven of that sin of divorce, does God still remember it against him or her? Well then, if God has forgiven and forgotten the divorce, where does that leave the divorced person? What is his or her classification in the eyes of God? Single? If a person is not married, then he or she must be single. What was your classification before you got married? Single? Isn't that what you wrote or checked on application forms? Well, a single person doesn't get *re*married, he just gets married!

In Harmony with God

Notice verse 28 again: **But and if thou marry, thou hast not sinned; and if a virgin marry, she hath not sinned.** In other words, it is no more of a sin for a divorced person to marry than it is for a virgin to marry. Neither of the two commits sin by getting married.

If you have trouble with this concept, take another look at the woman at the well. She had been married five times, and was living with a man to whom she was not married. Jesus pointed out that fact to her Himself. Yet He did not condemn her, nor did He say that she was being unfaithful to her (first and only) husband. On the contrary, He said she had been *married* five times. Jesus recognized the possibility of a person's being married more than once in life. So should His Church.

Jesus did not tell this woman that He could forgive, but that He would never forget. That is another "tradition of men." Someone has said that anyone who says he has forgiven but will never forget, never forgave to begin with. That is true. Webster's Dictionary gives several definitions of the word "forgive." One of them is: "To give up resentment against...." Unless that feeling of resentment is removed, forgiveness has not taken place. Jesus forgave this woman (just as He forgave the woman taken in the very act of adultery). As a result, she led a whole city to the Lord.

I wonder what would happen in the lives of divorced people if the Church of Jesus Christ would do for them what Jesus Christ Himself did for this divorced person. There are some divorced people in this nation right now who are mighty in ministry for the Lord. They are sweeping hundreds of people into the Kingdom of God. Thank God, He forgives. Would to God His children did!

Now please don't misunderstand. I am not advocating divorce. I am not advocating remarriage. What I am advocating is forgiveness.

And I am also not, as some would say, "giving people a license to get a divorce." They don't need a license. Certainly not from me. People were doing that for hundreds of years before I ever came on the scene. And it's likely they will be doing that long after I'm gone. I am not in the "divorce-license-granting" business. In fact, I am not in business at all. Like all Christians, I am in the ministry, the ministry of reconciliation: "that by word and deed we might aim to bring others into harmony with Him...(who is) not counting up and holding against [men] their trespasses [but cancelling them]" (2 Cor. 5:18,19 AMP).

"Well, that's all well and good," you might say, "but what about Jesus' statement that if a person marries someone who is divorced, that person commits adultery?"

I've already pointed out that if anyone marries a divorced person, he or she automatically becomes involved in the spiritual turmoil in that life.

Look at verse 28 again. **...Nevertheless such shall have trouble in the flesh.** That word flesh is not referring to the physical body. It is the very same word that is used in the fifth chapter of Galatians in reference to "the works of the flesh." Paul is really saying the same thing that Jesus said, "If you have been divorced and you marry again, you are going to have trouble in the flesh." Why? Because of the spiritual disruption in which you are getting yourself involved.

Divorced and remarried people have enough trouble to contend with as it is, they don't need the Church to add more. As Christians, that is precisely what we have been doing. God has not given us the ministry of retribution, but of reconciliation. Our mission is "to bring others into *harmony* with Him."

The Time Is Short

But this I say, brethren, the time is short: it remaineth, that both they that have wives be as though they had none;

And they that weep, as though they wept not; and they that rejoice, as though they rejoiced not; and they that buy, as though they possessed not;

And they that use this world, as not abusing it: for the fashion of this world passeth away.

But I would have you without carefulness. He that is unmarried careth for the things that belong to the Lord, how he may please the Lord:

But he that is married careth for the things that are of the world, how he may please his wife.

There is difference also between a wife and a virgin. The unmarried woman careth for the things of the Lord, that she may be holy both in body and in spirit: but she that is married careth for the things of the world, how she may please her husband.

And this I speak for your own profit; not that I may cast a snare upon you, but for that which is comely, and that ye may attend upon the Lord without distraction.

1 Corinthians 7:29-35

Paul was telling these people that all these things we have been discussing were distracting them from their purpose in being born again—which is, of course, to serve the Lord and spread His Gospel. I believe that is true today. For too long the Church has been distracted by *issues*. We need desperately to get back to our *commission*. Whether we are single, married, divorced, or remarried, we need to put all these things behind us and focus our attention upon the Lord and all our efforts upon His mission. Let's not become so entangled in personal matters, so engrossed in material concerns, so wrapped up in accumulating possessions and following the fashions of this world, that we neglect our calling. Let's take this world for Jesus!

That was Paul's point all along. That really was the point Jesus was making. That is my point in this whole study. The real, burning issue of the Church of Jesus Christ today is not divorce, remarriage or adultery, it is fidelity—faithfulness to the One Who created us, called us, and commissioned us. The time is short. Let's not waste anymore of it on controversy. Let's leave all of those things to the theologians to debate. Let us be about our Father's business!

Free from the Law

But if any man think that he behaveth himself uncomely toward his virgin, and if she pass the flower of her age, and need so require, let him do what he will, he sinneth not: let them marry.

Nevertheless he that standeth stedfast in his heart, having no necessity, but hath power over his own will, and hath so decreed in his heart that he will keep his virgin, doeth well.

So then he that giveth her in marriage doeth well; but he that giveth her not in marriage doeth better.

The wife is bound by the Law as long as her husband liveth; but if her husband be dead, she is at liberty to be married to whom she will; only in the Lord.

But she is happier if she so abide, after my judgment: and I think also that I have the Spirit of God.

1 Corinthians 7:36-40

So once again we see that Paul urges people to do as their own conscience leads them. If they feel led to get married, they do not sin if they do so. Likewise, if they think it best not to marry, that too is permissible.

But notice particularly verse 39: **The wife is bound by the Law as long as her husband liveth; but if her husband be dead, she is at liberty to be married to whom she will; only in the Lord.** That calls to mind what Paul said in Romans 7:1-4:

> **Know ye not, brethren, (for I speak to them that know the Law,) how that the Law hath dominion over a man as long as he liveth?**
>
> **For the woman which hath an husband is bound by the Law to her husband so long as he liveth; but if the husband be dead, she is loosed from the Law of her husband.**
>
> **So then if, while her husband liveth, she be married to another man, she shall be called an adulteress: but if her husband be dead, she is free from that law; so that she is no adulteress, though she be married to another man.**
>
> **Wherefore, my brethren, ye also are become dead to the Law by the body of Christ; that ye should be married to another, even to him who is raised from the dead, that we should bring forth fruit unto God.**

Question: To whom is Paul speaking here? To those who know the Law. And **...to them that know the law,...the law hath dominion over a man as long as he liveth.** The Law has dominion over a person as long as he or she lives. According to this scripture, according to the Law, if a man and a woman are married and then get a divorce, if that woman remarries, she is going to be called an adulteress. Who is going to call her that? Those who know the Law and live by it. But please notice that Paul did not say that she *shall* be an adulteress, only that she shall be *called* an adulteress.

Yet if her husband dies, she is free to remarry whom she will, without fear of being labeled an adulteress. Do you realize what that means? It means that we have more confidence in the death of a husband to free a woman from the Law than we do in the death, burial and resurrection of our Lord Jesus Christ to free her from that same Law! If a woman's husband dies, we say she is free of the Law. But a person is not set free from the Law because of the death of a spouse, but because of the death on the cross of the Lord Jesus Christ! "Wherefore, my brethren, *ye also are become dead to the Law by the body of Christ.*" So says Paul. Because of what Jesus has done for us on Calvary, you and I are forever free of the Law, thank God!

Therefore Glorify God

> Marriage is honourable in all, and the bed undefiled: but whoremongers and adulterers God will judge.
>
> **Hebrews 13:4**

According to God's Word, marriage is honorable in all. Does that include all marriages, even remarriages? Does all mean all? Marriage, whether the first or the fiftieth, is honorable and should be viewed as such.

> Now the Spirit speaketh expressly, that in the latter times some shall depart from the faith, giving heed to seducing spirits, and doctrines of devils;
>
> Speaking lies in hypocrisy; having their conscience seared with a hot iron;
>
> Forbidding to marry, and commanding to abstain from meats, which God hath created to be received

with thanksgiving of them which believe and know the truth.

For every creature of God is good, and nothing to be refused, if it be received with thanksgiving.

1 Timothy 4:1-4

Paul said there would be those who would forbid to marry. They are with us today. Many, many churches and Christians forbid divorced people to remarry. Paul called such teachings "doctrines of devils."

But doesn't the Bible indicate in Deuteronomy 24 that divorced people are unclean?

Perhaps it does give that impression. And they are "unclean." Ceremonially unclean according to Jewish Law. But most Christians today are not Orthodox Jews.

According to 1 Timothy 4:4, ...**every creature of God is good.** Is a Christian a "creature of God"? Even a divorced or remarried Christian? Remember 1 Corinthians 6:11? ...**But ye** (Christians) **are washed, but ye are sanctified, but ye are justified in the name of the Lord Jesus, and by the Spirit of our God.**

I earnestly believe that what the Lord is saying to us in this whole lesson is simply what He told the Apostle Peter: "What I have cleansed, you are not to call unclean!" (Acts 10:15.) Peter learned that lesson well, for in that same chapter he testified: **God hath shewed me that I should not call** *any man* **common or unclean** (v. 28).

Let's also learn that lesson. Let's remember that every creature of God is good. Let's turn our attention from "giving heed to seducing spirits" and devote it to proclaiming "the message of reconciliation—of the restoration of favor."

As Pastor of Family Worship Center in Tulsa, Oklahoma, Dr. Ken Stewart is very conscious of Satan's efforts to destroy marriages and lives. His extensive knowledge of God's Word is always presented in profound, yet practical, truths which have helped many to have meaningful lives and successful family relationships.

Dr. Stewart attended Brite Divinity School, Texas Christian University, where he received his Master of Divinity degree and his Doctor of Ministry degree.

He is the author of several books and teaching tape series and is in much demand as a speaker, traveling throughout this country and abroad ministering God's Word.

For a complete list of tapes and
books by Dr. Stewart, write:

Family Worship Center
P. O. Box 690240
Tulsa, OK 74169

*Feel free to include your prayer requests
and comments when you write.*